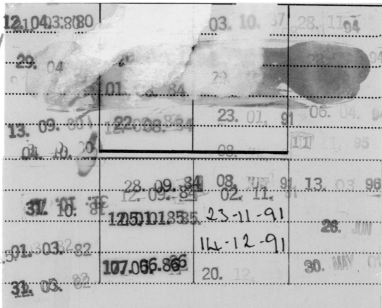

LONDON BOROUGH OF

Wandsworth

15

PUTNEY LIBRARY
DISRAELI ROAD SW15 2DR
01-788 2341

Early Closing Thursday

THIS BOOK SHOULD BE RETURNED ON OR BEFORE THE
LATEST DATE SHOWN ON THIS LABEL OR THE CARD
INSERTED IN THE POCKET.

Rigoletto

MASTERWORKS
OF OPERA

General Editor: Charles Osborne

CHARLES OSBORNE

Rigoletto

A GUIDE TO THE OPERA

FOREWORD BY
TITO GOBBI

BARRIE & JENKINS
COMMUNICA - EUROPA

Designed and produced by Breslich & Foss, London

© Breslich & Foss 1979

First published in 1979 by Barrie & Jenkins
24 Highbury Crescent, London N5 1RX

Design: Craig Dodd
Picture Research: Philippa Lewis

Filmset and printed in Great Britain by
BAS Printers Limited, Over Wallop, Hampshire

ISBN 0 214 20654 8

Contents

Foreword by Tito Gobbi

Young people have fast and abrupt reactions that age and wisdom tend to smooth down. Still, they are beautiful natural impulses. At the beginning of my career, I once attended a very poor performance of *Rigoletto*. The singing, though professional, had no meaning, and the loud voice of the leading performer was unable to express the character's feelings. The acting was disgraceful and the make-up primitive. I was about to make an energetic protest and stood up, but was checked immediately by thunderous applause which brought my young brain into confusion. Then I understood; it was the opera itself, and not the performance, that had carried the audience away. *Rigoletto* is indestructible!

After that early unfortunate experience, I promised myself that I would study this noble work in all its genuine truth, never degrading it with vocal or theatrical gimmicks. I faithfully followed Verdi's advice always to study and meditate deeply on the subject, and I started with my usual practice which was to sketch and make a model of the character so that I could see him physically before my eyes. I am always fascinated by the wonderful job of compiling a sort of dossier, avidly searching and reading whatever I can about the personage and his time, his costumes, his surroundings. I want to know the way he walks as a jester or as a father, how he laughs, how he cries. I must get to know him so thoroughly as to *become* him. I started asking myself all the *whys* for each phrase or situation until I could find the right answers.

Some rapid expression or musical passage, some slight piece of action which seems to end almost before it has begun, these are things which are quite often sadly neglected. And yet they are of vital importance to the development of a drama in which the mutation of the feelings is so very dynamic.

In *Rigoletto* Verdi has described everything for the intelligent interpreter, and the invaluable treasures which I discovered as I studied both excited and astonished me. Thus, I acquired the habit of studying a score in its entirety, in order to become acquainted with every role and be able to build my own more faithfully. And I could see, looking into the inner soul of each character in the score of *Rigoletto*, that all of them are real people.

Every time I sang the role of the jester whose love for his daughter is the overwhelming passion of his life, I honestly and devotedly gave myself to the exacting task of penetrating Rigoletto's continuous changes of feeling. I followed the thoughts of his deranged mind, and I lived and suffered his immense tragedy. I seem to be speaking always about interpretation, but to me singing and acting are a whole and must go perfectly together. *Rigoletto* is strenuous both vocally and dramatically, and the 'actor-singer', as Verdi says (note the word 'actor' comes first) must try not to become emotionally involved. This is dangerous, and sometimes exhausting for the voice. I used to have a good 'cry-out' at rehearsals so that I knew how far I could go. Severe self-control is needed in heart-rending moments such as the one in Act II when poor Rigoletto enters, pretending to jest with the courtiers, then going from tears to laughter and then to the fury of the Vendetta.

I enjoyed tremendously the powerful recitatives of the last act, feeling myself swept onward by the storm and the wind to the tragic end. It took me a good ten years before I dared to sing the role of Rigoletto for the first time at the Royal Opera House, Covent Garden in 1956. Many years later, after some three hundred and seventy performances of the role, I realized I could no longer give it my best vocally. Nor could I stand the physical strain, and I sadly said good-bye to my stage Rigoletto. But I continue to love the opera, and study it even more deeply as my experience grows. I feel fortunate to be able to pass on something of what I have learned to younger singers, through my activities as producer and teacher.

I wish Charles Osborne the greatest success in presenting this masterpiece of Verdi, as he sheds new light on the work and presents further aspects of it to guide and delight all who love *Rigoletto*.

8

Rigoletto

OPERA IN THREE ACTS BY
GIUSEPPE VERDI
LIBRETTO BY FRANCESCO MARIA PIAVE

Background to the Opera

Although Verdi composed *Rigoletto* at the beginning of 1851, he had first considered using Victor Hugo's play, *Le roi s'amuse*, seven years earlier, for it is included in a list of possible subjects for operas which he jotted down in 1844 in his *Copialettere* or notebooks in which he kept copies of business correspondence. His list begins with three Shakespeare plays—*King Lear*, *Hamlet* and *The Tempest*—none of which Verdi was to use, though he wrote operas on *Macbeth* and *The Merry Wives of Windsor*. The fourth and fifth titles on the list are Byron's *Cain* and Hugo's *Le roi s'amuse*, and there are other plays by Hugo, Dumas, Grillparzer, Calderón, Racine and so on. Other than *Le roi s'amuse*, the only one actually to become a Verdi opera was Werner's *Attila*.

Le roi s'amuse next surfaced in Verdi's mind in 1849. In a letter to Vincenzo Flauto, impresario of the Teatro San Carlo, Naples, in September of that year, he wrote:

> Now we must give serious thought to the libretto of the opera to be produced after Easter, for, to ensure that everything proceeds smoothly, Cammarano will need to have prepared a rough draft and to have sent me the first pieces by the end of October, when this Eloisa [*Luisa Miller*] will be staged and I shall be leaving Naples for a while, so I should like to take with me the text to be set. As a subject, suggest *Le roi s'amuse* by Victor Hugo to Cammarano. A beautiful play with tremendous dramatic situations, and containing two magnificent roles for Frezzolini and De Bassini.

Verdi travelled to Naples the following month to stage his opera *Luisa Miller*, whose libretto had been written by Salvatore Cammarano on a play by Schiller, but although the opera was a success Verdi was not happy in his relations with the

management, and he left Naples vowing he would never produce another opera there. *Le roi s'amuse* retreated into the background again, and Verdi's next opera after *Luisa Miller* was *Stiffelio*, written for the Teatro Grande, Trieste, and produced there in November 1850. The librettist of *Stiffelio* was Francesco Maria Piave, the Venetian poet with whom Verdi had already collaborated on four operas, *Ernani*, *I due Foscari*, *Macbeth* and *Il corsaro*. (Though Verdi also pursued for a time the idea of writing another work with Cammarano, the subject they corresponded about was not *Le roi s'amuse* but *King Lear*, an opera which was never to be written.)

In 1850 Verdi received commissions to write two operas working with Piave as librettist in both cases. *Stiffelio* having been agreed upon, based on *Le Pasteur* by Eugène Bourgeois and Émile Souvestre, Verdi proceeded to compose it quickly for the opera house at Trieste. The second contract was with the Teatro Fenice, Venice, where Verdi's earlier operas *Ernani* and *Attila* had been given their premières. Here there were difficulties to be surmounted concerning the choice of subject. Negotiations had been begun by the Fenice Theatre in a letter to Verdi on March 9, 1850, signed by the theatre's President, C. D. Marzari, and Secretary, G. Brenna:

> Desirous of giving the Venetian public the opportunity to admire a new work by your distinguished musical genius, I beg you to inform me if you have any commitments for the forthcoming 1850–51 season from Carnival to Lent. If you have not, would you also be so kind as to let me know if you would be willing to undertake to write an *opera seria* for this theatre, and on what terms.
>
> The management would prefer to leave ownership of the opera in your hands, agreeing to pay a rental fee for the material for the first production in this theatre.
>
> Should, however, the retention of ownership prove to be an obstacle to settling the contract, the management would be willing to retain the work itself, or have it made over to the impresario. But, when setting out your terms, the management begs you to bear in mind that current circumstances have considerably reduced the resources of Venice and that, in consequence, this theatre can no longer afford the fees it was able to agree on other occasions.

Verdi replied on March 14:

> Most flattered by your request, I hasten to reply, especially as I have not a great deal of time to spend in negotiations. In fact, I ask that you do all that you can to let me have an answer before Easter. Here are my terms.
>
> (i)   the score to remain my property, with the management to have the right to produce the work during Lent, 1851, at the Teatro La Fenice only.
>
> (ii) the libretto to be provided at my expense.
>
> (iii) the opera to have its first performance at the beginning of Lent, which will oblige me to be in Venice twenty days in advance.

    (iv)   dress rehearsal with scenery and costumes as for the première (either in private or with an audience, as the management prefers).

    (v)   the management to pay me the sum of six thousand Austrian lire, half upon my arrival in Venice, and half on the day of the dress rehearsal.

Again I beg of you to be so kind as to reply as soon as possible. My only other stipulation is that the contract should not be signed until I know the names of the principal artists.

Without waiting for a reply from the Fenice, Verdi now wrote to Piave informing him of the terms he had suggested to the management, and asking the librettist to begin thinking about a subject. In a postscript, he adds: 'Have a look at a Spanish play, *Gusmano il Buono*'. But the Fenice's offer, when it arrived, was three thousand lire, only half the sum Verdi had stipulated. Indignant letters from Busseto were dispatched to the Fenice and to Piave. To Piave: 'So they won't pay a few thousand lire more, for an opera written expressly for them? What about the libretto? What about my expenses? All things being equal, I'd prefer coming to Venice to writing an opera elsewhere; I'd even be happy to make some sacrifice, but I see no reason to turn down better offers. . . .' And to Brenna, the Fenice's Secretary: 'The request I made was very reasonable, since I'd taken into consideration the circumstances and the times. I couldn't even accept five thousand Austrian lire with the theatre having the right to perform the work in future seasons, because this condition would deprive me of three or four thousand francs which I would get from the publisher to whom I would give the score. Add to this, *inter nos*, that the company engaged is not at all to my liking.'

The President (Marzari) and Secretary (Brenna) both wrote, separately, to Verdi on April 10. 'For the pleasure of obtaining for Venice a completely new work by the foremost Italian composer of our time, I throw all considerations of economy to the winds and agree to the six thousand Austrian lire', said the President, asking only that the Fenice be allowed the right to produce the work again in later seasons ('a right which, however, cannot be to your detriment since it is only very rarely that the theatre makes use of it'). And the Secretary promised: 'As to the company, tell me in confidence which artist you would like to have replaced, and I'll do everything possible to oblige you'.

Verdi wrote a gracious acceptance on April 18, and undertook to begin rehearsals in Venice on February 1, 1851. 'I don't lose much time orchestrating and rehearsing', he told Marzari, 'so the management may rest assured that, if rehearsals start on time, the première can take place around February 20.' On the same day, Verdi also wrote to Brenna, asking him to pass on a message to Piave to the effect that, should Piave not find a copy of the Spanish play (*Guzmán el bueno*, to give it its original title), he should look at *Kean*, 'which is one of Dumas' best plays'.

The Fenice management proved less than keen on *Kean*, and in correspondence with Piave, Verdi considered and dismissed a number of other possibilities. In a letter of April 28 from Verdi to Piave, *Le roi s'amuse* surfaced again:

As to the genre, it matters little to me whether it's grandiose, passionate, fantastic, as long as it's good, although the passionate is safer. Make use of all the characters that the subject calls for. . . . We'll have trouble finding anything better than *Gusmano il buono*. However, I've got another subject which, if the police will agree to allow its performance, could be one of the greatest works of art in the modern theatre. Who knows? They allowed *Ernani*, so they might allow this too, and there are no conspiracies in it.

Try it! The subject is great, immense, and includes a character who is one of the greatest creations to be found in the theatre of all countries and of all times. The subject is *Le roi s'amuse*, and the character I'm talking about is Triboulet; if Varesi is engaged it couldn't be better for him or for us.

P.S. As soon as you get this letter, race about the town on all fours and find some influential person who can get us permission to do *Le roi s'amuse*. Don't doze off; shake yourself awake; hurry. I shall expect you at Busseto, but not now, after they've agreed to the subject.

A few days later, Verdi wrote again to Piave:

Oh, *Le roi s'amuse* is the greatest subject and perhaps the greatest play of modern times. Triboulet is a creation worthy

PUBLIÉ PAR EUGÈNE RENDUEL,

M DCCC XXXII.

ABOVE: Title-page of the first edition of Hugo's Le roi s'amuse *(Paris, 1832). Drawing by Johannot*

of Shakespeare!! Like *Ernani*, it's a subject that can't fail. You remember six years ago, when Mocenigo suggested *Ernani* to me, I exclaimed: 'Yes, by God that can't go wrong.' Now, in going over the various subjects, when *Le roi* came into my mind it was like a bolt of lightning, an inspiration, and I said the same thing, 'Yes, by God, that can't go wrong.' So, therefore, get the management interested, turn Venice upside down and talk the Censor into allowing this subject. Who cares if la Sanchioli is no good for it. If we had to pay attention to things like this, no operas would get written any more. For that matter, if everyone will allow me to say so, who are the certainties among today's singers? What happened on the first night of *Ernani* with the leading tenor of the day? What happened on the first night of *Foscari* with one of the leading companies of the day? Singers who are able to assure success by their very presence—Malibran, Rubini, Lablache, etc.—no longer exist.

Verdi continually urged Piave to stay as close as possible to the original in writing his libretto. ('Just stick to the French and you won't go wrong.') The librettist had his doubts about the division of the stage into two in the last act and also about the body in the sack, but Verdi knew his theatre and was confident that the scene would be dramatically effective. Clearly, the title would have to be changed, for it would not do to refer flippantly to monarchy. Verdi's first suggestion for an Italian title was *La maledizione* (The Curse).

The whole story lies in that curse which also becomes moral. An unhappy father who mourns the theft of his daughter's virtue is mocked by a court jester whom the father curses, and this curse lays hold of the jester in a dreadful way. This strikes me as moral and great to the highest degree. Take care that Saint-Vallier appears (as in the French) only twice, and that his words are few, emphatic and prophetic.

Piave came to Busseto to work on the libretto under Verdi's supervision and from Verdi's house he wrote to the Fenice management on August 5, 1850.

Verdi is dissatisfied with Sanchioli. He says it will be impossible to get anything out of her in that role, and that if she is in it the work will flop! He also adds that, if he had known he was to have Sanchioli who has never sung entire seasons in the big theatres, he would never have accepted the Venice commission. He also asks that you give this serious thought, as it is in our mutual interests.

The management now expressed a doubt whether the censorship would permit Hugo's play to be used as the basis of an opera, and Verdi at once sent Piave back to Venice with a letter for the theatre's President:

The doubt you express as to whether *Le roi s'amuse* will be allowed puts me in a very embarrassing position. I was assured by Piave that there would be no difficulty with this subject. Trusting his word, I began to study and consider it deeply, and the entire idea and the musical colour of it were already formed in my mind. I could say that the greater part of the work has already been done. If I were now required to turn to another subject, I wouldn't have enough time at my disposal for the required study, and I should not be able to write an opera which would satisfy my artistic conscience.

By October, Piave had completed his libretto. He and Verdi were in Trieste for the rehearsals of *Stiffelio* when a letter arrived from Marzari asking for a copy of the libretto of *La maledizione* so that it could be forwarded to the censorship authority, the Direzione d'Ordine Pubblico, for approval. Early in December, the management of the Fenice received the following communication from the Director of the Ordine Pubblico:

His Excellency the Military Governor Chevalier Gorzkowski in his respected dispatch of the 26th instant N. 731 directs me to communicate to you his profound regret that the poet Piave and the celebrated Maestro Verdi should not have chosen a more worthy vehicle to display their talents than the revolting immorality and obscene triviality of the libretto of *La maledizione*, submitted to us for intended performance at the Teatro Fenice.

His above-mentioned Excellency has decided that the performance shall be absolutely forbidden, and wishes me at the same time to request you not to make further enquiries in this matter. I am returning the manuscript sent to me with your accompanying letter of the 20th instant N. 18.

Verdi, by this time back at home in Busseto, was furious with the authorities and with Piave. He wrote to the Fenice President, Marzari, on December 5:

The letter which arrived with the decree completely banning *La maledizione* was so unexpected that I almost went out of my mind. In this matter, Piave was at fault: completely at fault! He assured me in several letters, written as long ago as

ABOVE: *The auditorium of the Teatro Fenice, Venice, where* Rigoletto *was first produced*

May, that approval had been obtained for it. This being so, I set to music a large part of the play, working with the greatest zeal in order to finish at the time agreed. The decree forbidding it drives me to desperation, because now it is too late to choose another libretto. It would be impossible, absolutely impossible, for me to set another subject to music this winter. This was the third time I was granted the honour of writing for Venice, and the management knows with what punctuality I have always carried out my duties. It knows that when I was almost dying I gave my word I would finish *Attila*, and I did so. Now I repeat on my oath that it is impossible for me to set a new libretto, even if I were to slave away to the point of endangering my health. Nevertheless, to demonstrate my good will, I offer the only thing that I can do. *Stiffelio* is an opera new to Venice. I suggest presenting it, and I would myself come to produce it at whatever time the management thinks opportune, during the carnival season of 1850–51. There is in this opera one very great difficulty (also due to the censor), and that is the final scene. It cannot be staged as it is; but if it is not possible to obtain permission from Vienna to do it as I intended, I would be willing to change the ending, which would thus be completely new for Venice. I request the management to accept this proof of my good will, and to believe that the damage and displeasure I am caused by this prohibition are greater than I have words to describe.

Marzari did not want to be fobbed off with an opera written for and already performed in Trieste, so he and Piave continued their struggle with the censor. It was hardly surprising that the Austrian authorities (Venice at this time being part of the Austrian Empire and administered from Vienna) should object to a play which showed a reigning monarch as debauched and conscienceless; even if the civil authority had not objected to this aspect of the plot, religious proprieties would have been offended by a curse being worked out on stage and also by action which was, by the standards of the time, immoral and obscene. Piave, without consulting Verdi, submitted to the authorities a revised libretto in which the King, Francis I, became a Duke of Vendôme, and in which the action was considerably bowdlerized. When Verdi saw it, he rejected it outright: 'In order to reply immediately to yours of the 11th,' he wrote to Marzari on December 14:

> Let me say I have had very little time to examine the new libretto. I have seen enough, however, to know that in its present form it lacks character, significance, and, in short, the dramatic moments leave one completely cold. If it was necessary to change the characters' names, then the locality should have been changed as well. You could have a Duke or Prince of some other place, for example a Pier Luigi Farnese, or put the action back to a time before Louis XI when France was not a united kingdom, and have a Duke of Burgundy or Normandy etc. etc., but in any case an absolute ruler. In the fifth scene of Act I, all that anger of the courtiers against Triboletto doesn't make sense. The old man's curse, so terrifying and sublime in the original, here becomes ridiculous because his motive for uttering the curse doesn't have the same significance and because it is no longer a subject who speaks in so forthright a manner to his King.

LEFT: *Cover of a piano reduction of Emile Tavan's* Grand Fantasy for Orchestra on Rigoletto *(1921)*

Without this curse, what scope or significance does the drama have? The Duke has no character. The Duke must definitely be a libertine: without this, there is no justification for Triboletto's fear that his daughter might leave her hiding-place, and the drama is made impossible. What would the Duke be doing in the last act, alone in a remote inn, without an invitation, without a rendezvous? I don't understand why the sack has gone. Why should a sack matter to the police? Are they worried about the effect? But let me say this: why do they think they know better than I do about this? Who is playing the maestro? Who can say this will make an effect and that won't? We had this kind of difficulty with the horn in *Ernani.* Well, did anyone laugh at the sound of that horn? With that sack removed, it is improbable that Triboletto would talk for half an hour to a corpse, before a flash of lightning reveals it to be his daughter. Finally, I see that they have avoided making Triboletto an ugly hunchback!! A hunchback who sings? Why not? Will it be effective? I don't

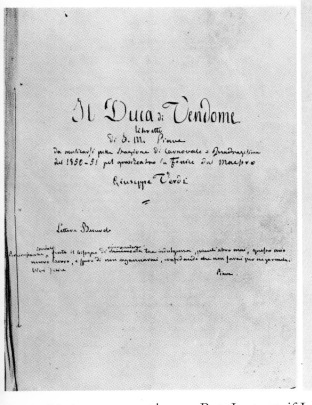

know. But, I repeat, if I don't know, then they who propose this change don't know either. I thought it would be beautiful to portray this extremely deformed and ridiculous character who is inwardly passionate and full of love. I chose the subject precisely because of these qualities and these original traits, and if they are cut I shall no longer be able to set it to music. If anyone says to me I can leave my notes as they are for this new plot, I reply that I don't inderstand this kind of thinking, and I say frankly that my music, whether beautiful or ugly, is never written in a vacuum, and that I always try to give it character.

To sum up, an original, powerful drama has been turned into something ordinary and cold. I am extremely sorry that the management did not reply to my last letter. I can only repeat and beg them to do what I asked then, because my artistic conscience will not allow me to set this libretto to music.

Piave and Brenna, the Fenice's Secretary, visited Verdi in Busseto, and persuaded him to accept a compromise by which the situations in Hugo's play were, for the most part, left intact, only the locale and the names of the characters being changed. The agreed changes were noted in a document drawn up 'at the residence of Maestro Giuseppe Verdi' on December 30, 1850:

> In accordance with the contract received on 27th December from the President of the Board of Management of the Teatro La Fenice, the undersigned Secretary of the President invites Maestro Verdi to specify the changes which he consents to make in the libretto submitted under the title of *La maledizione*, in order that this libretto may be composed for the current season, Carnival and Lent 1850–51, according to the contract of April 23rd. The changes are made in order to remove the objections which the State authorities place in the way of its performance.
>
> In consultation, therefore, with the poet Francesco Maria Piave, the following is agreed:
>
> 1. The scene shall be changed from the French court to that of an independent Duke of Burgundy or Normandy, or to the court of a minor absolutist Italian state, preferably that of Pier Luigi Farnese, and in the period most suitable for scenic and dramatic effect.
>
> 2. The original characters of the drama *Le roi s'amuse* by Victor Hugo shall be retained, but other names shall be found for them, dependent on the period chosen.
>
> 3. The scene in which Francesco is shown determined to use the key in his possession to enter the room of the abducted Bianca shall be omitted. It shall be replaced by another which preserves the decencies, but does not detract from the interest of the play.
>
> 4. The King or Duke shall come to the rendezvous in Magellona's tavern as the result of a pretended invitation brought to him by the Triboletto character.
>
> 5. In the scene in which the sack containing the corpse of Triboletto's daughter appears, Maestro Verdi reserves to himself the right to make such changes as he considers necessary.
>
> 6. The above mentioned changes require more time than was originally supposed. Therefore Maestro Verdi declares

fresco by Andrea
Mantegna, of the
Ducal Palace in
Mantua, home of
Vincenzo Gonzaga,
the infamous Duke of
Mantua

the new opera cannot be performed before February 28th or March 1st.

Accordingly, this document has been signed and agreed upon by those present: G. Verdi, F. M. Piave, G. Brenna (Secretary)

The censor agreed to these suggestions, and the names of the characters were changed to those by which we know them today. Francis I, King of France became the Duke of Mantua. Although he was not named more exactly, he was understood to be the infamous Vincenzo Gonzaga. (As Piave said to Verdi, 'By now, everyone knows who was ruling at that time.') Verdi and Piave may have been aware that a French play, *Rigoletti, ou le dernier des fous*, had been produced in Paris in 1835, or that there was a character called Rigolette in *Les mystères de Paris* (1842). Whether they were or not, their Triboulet (Triboletto) became Rigoletto, from the French *rigoler*, to guffaw, and the opera now took its title from him. Verdi proceeded to complete his score.

24

He is said to have written *Rigoletto* in forty days, but the opera had been in his head for several months and parts of the music had already been written down.

At its première in Venice on March 11, 1851, *Rigoletto* was an enormous success, and it has remained one of the world's most popular operas ever since. Soon after the Venice performances it was being played all over Italy, though in order to gain acceptance with various local censors it was produced under a variety of titles, among them *Viscardello*, *Clara di Perth* and *Lionello*, the names of characters and locales appropriately changed. In its first Paris season in 1857, *Rigoletto* was performed more than one hundred times. Not surprisingly, Victor Hugo resented its popularity, but when he finally heard the opera he was forced to admit its greatness. Of the famous quartet, '*Bella figlia dell' amore*', he exclaimed, somewhat ambiguously: 'If I could only make four characters in my plays speak at the same time, and have the audience grasp the words and sentiments, I would obtain the very same effect.'

ABOVE: *Poster announcing the first performance of* Rigoletto *at the Teatro La Fenice, 10 March, 1851*

25

Rigoletto's immediate success was with audiences, not necessarily with critics. The *Gazzetta di Venezia* could not make up its mind immediately after the Venice première:

An opera like this cannot be judged after one evening. Yesterday we were, so to speak, overwhelmed by the novelty of it all—the novelty, or rather the strangeness of the subject, the novelty of the music, the style, the very form of the numbers. . . . The composer and the poet . . . have searched for their ideal of beauty in the horrible, the deformed. To achieve their effects they have had recourse not to the usual emotions of passion and terror but to those of anguish and horror. Frankly we cannot praise their taste in these matters.

Despite all this, however, the opera had the most complete success, and the composer was acclaimed, applauded and called for after almost every number, two of which had to be repeated. And, to be truthful, the orchestration is admirable, marvellous; this orchestra speaks and weeps with you, and arouses your every passion. . . . Less admirable, however, is the writing for the voice. Notably as regards the lack of important concerted numbers, this departs from the current style. One quartet and a trio near the end, in which it is difficult to grasp completely the musical thought, and that is all.

After the first Milan performance at La Scala in 1853, *L'Italia musicale* said the opera was unsatisfactory because of its absolute and complete lack of melody. A similar comment was made by the *Gazette musicale* of Paris ('*La partition est pauvre de mélodies*') The London *Times* hated it: 'The imitations and plagiarism from other composers are frequent. . . . In aiming at simplicity, Signor Verdi has hit frivolity. . . . He has very few ideas that can be pronounced original . . . the most feeble opera of Signor Verdi with which we have the advantage to be acquainted. . . . Analysis would be a loss of time and space.' The London *Morning Post* concurred: 'Our opinion of Signor Verdi's powers is well known; and as his present work is rather worse than better than previous productions by him, which we have already condemned, it will be unnecessary to enter into painful details. This opera is certainly not so noisy as *Ernani*, *Attila*, *Masnadieri* or *Anato* [*Nabucco*], but it contains other grievous faults, for which the mere absence of 'row' cannot compensate.'

On the other hand, Signor Verdi, normally the most gloomily self-critical of composers, thought it his best opera: he expressed this opinion in a letter to a friend four years after the première. He also thought it 'revolutionary', and 'the best subject as regards theatrical effect that I've ever set to music'. To his first Rigoletto, Felice Varesi, he said that he never expected to do better than the quartet.

LEFT: *Felice Varesi (1813–89) who sang the title role and Teresa Brambilla (1813–95) who sang Gilda in the first production of* Rigoletto

From Le roi s'amuse to Rigoletto

Le roi s'amuse, the play by Victor Hugo upon which *Rigoletto* is based, was conceived and written within three weeks, in June, 1832. The French poet, novelist and playwright had, in 1827 at the age of twenty-five, become the undisputed leader of the romantic movement in France, with the publication of the preface to his drama, *Cromwell*, a manifesto of romanticism, asserting the independence of the playwright from the rigid rules of classicism. Throughout the nineteenth century, a number of Hugo's plays were used by composers as the bases of operas: *Angelo* (1835) served for both Mercadante's *Il giuramento* (1837) and Ponchielli's *La Gioconda* (1876); *Marion de Lorme*, *Lucrèce Borgia*, *Ruy Blas*, all became operas. Verdi's *Ernani* (1884) is based on Hugo's *Hernani* (1830). In English-speaking countries, it is Hugo's novels which are his best-known works, among them *The Hunchback of Notre Dame* and *Les Misérables*.

A romantic and liberal idealist, Hugo played an active, though admittedly not greatly influential part in French political life. After first serving as a peer under the monarchy of Louis Philippe, he transferred his loyalty to the republicans in 1848 and was elected to the popular assembly. At the restoration of the Second Empire, Hugo fled the country in 1851 and lived in exile for eighteen years in the Channel Islands. So, at the time the military authorities in Venice were considering the Teatro Fenice's request to produce an opera based on a play by Hugo, the playwright was regarded as a potentially dangerous anti-monarchist.

Le roi s'amuse had, in any case, fallen foul of political censorship on its first production in Paris in 1832. Three days before the première, a pistol-shot had been fired at the King, Louis Philippe as he was crossing the Pont Royal on his way to the Chambre. Paris was in a state of unrest, and in the theatre the claque which Hugo had assembled was finding it difficult to

whip up the audience's enthusiasm for the play. A degree of excitement was generated when the jester Triboulet rounded on the courtiers of Francis I with the snarled accusation: '*Vos mères aux laquais se sont prostituées! Vous êtes tous bâtards!*' ('Your mothers have prostituted themselves to their lackeys! You are all bastards!'). A storm of protest arose from the boxes, countered by a chorus of the 'Marseillaise' from the young rebels in the pit. The following morning, the theatre was ordered to postpone any further performances of *Le roi s'amuse*, and two weeks later the play was formally banned. Its second performance was not to take place until fifty years later, in 1882, in the presence of the President of the Republic!

The French banned *Le roi s'amuse* on the grounds that it was an outrage to morality, though Hugo was surely right to protest that the real reason for the ban was that his play was seen as an incitement to rebellion. In a long preface to the play, which he wrote two weeks after the solitary first performance, he recounts the events leading up to the première, and then refutes the suggestion that the work is immoral:

The piece is immoral? Do you think so? Because of the subject? Look at the subject. Triboulet is deformed, Triboulet is ill, Triboulet is a court buffoon: a threefold misery which makes him evil. Triboulet hates the King because he is the King, the noblemen because they are noblemen, and mankind because they have no humps on their backs. His only pastime is unceasingly to incite the nobles against the King, crushing the weaker with the stronger. He depraves the King, he corrupts him, he stultifies him; he encourages him in tyranny, in ignorance, in vice; he directs his attention to all the well-born families, continually pointing out to him a wife to seduce, a sister to abduct, a daughter to dishonour. In the hands of Triboulet, the King is merely an all-powerful puppet ruining the lives of all those among whom the jester sets him down to play.

One day, during a banquet, at the very moment when Triboulet is urging the King to abduct the wife of M. de Cossé, M. de Saint-Vallier forces himself into the King's presence and, in a loud voice, reproaches him for having dishonoured Diane de Poitiers. This father, from whom the King has taken his daughter, is jeered at and insulted by Triboulet. Raising his arm, the father curses Triboulet. It is from this that the entire play develops. The real subject of the drama is *the curse of M. de Saint-Vallier*.

Hugo then proceeds to take the reader through *Le roi s'amuse*, act by act, challenging him to find anything obscene or offensive in the entire play. ('We repeat expressly that we are not now addressing the police, for we would not do them so much honour, but that part of the public to whom this discussion may seem necessary.') He desires art to be chaste, he says, but not prudish (*'l'art chaste, et non l'art prude'*). A few paragraphs further on, he quotes words he had written the previous year in his preface to *Marion de Lorme*: 'It is precisely when there is no censorship that authors must censor themselves, honestly, conscientiously, severely. It is thus that they raise the dignity of art. When one has complete liberty, it behoves one to keep within bounds.'

The situation in Paris in 1832, as described by Hugo in this preface, is the classical one of the revolution which consolidates itself by taking on some of the aspects of the régime it has deposed. In July, 1830, says Hugo, France made great and sudden advances towards liberty, towards civilization. But the government was barely thirty months old, and was exhibiting 'the little furies of childhood' ('*petites fureurs d'enfant*'). He sees 1832 as a time of political transition, a moment of general weariness when acts of despotism are possible, even in a society infiltrated by ideas of emancipation and liberty. Two years ago, he says, one feared for order, and now one trembles for liberty. Questions of free thought, intelligence and art are 'imperiously quelled by the viziers of the king of the barricades'.

The principal characters in *Le roi s'amuse* are quite clearly and indisputably based on historical personages, and even minor characters who are barely sketched in are still given real historical names. But, although Hugo liked to think there was historical fact beneath the poetry and drama of his play, the evidence, such as it is, does not support him. Francis I was born in 1494, became King of France in 1515, and died in 1547. (Hugo's play is set in the 1520s, when the King was still a young man.) Hugo portrays him as a libertine, and also asserts in his preface that 'history allowed us to show you Francis I drunk in the hovels of the rue du Pélican', but fails to be more specific, and appears not to be supported by historians. History certainly suggests that Francis was quite fond of the ladies, but the French historian Brantôme praises him for having introduced 'young women of distinction' into his court which prior to his time had been a 'convocation and habitation of harlots', and also tells us that 'among his other virtues, the king was a great lover of good literature and scholarly men'.

LEFT: *Victor Hugo's sketch at the end of the manuscript of* Le roi s'amuse, *entitled* 'Le dernier bouffon songeant au dernier roi'

The historical Triboulet, jester to the court of Louis XII and Francis I, is said to have had 'a low forehead and big eyes, big hooked nose, stomach flat and long, and a back high enough to carry a basket', but not to resemble Hugo's Triboulet in any other aspect. Nor is Hugo's Saint-Vallier any closer to history. In *Le roi s'amuse* Saint-Vallier, father of Diane de Poitiers, forces his way into the court festivities in Act I to confront Francis I and accuse him of a monstrous outrage:

> You, François de Valois, on the evening of that day, without fear, pity, decency or love, in your bed, that tomb of women's virtue, did coldly, through your vile kisses, tarnish, soil, blight, dishonour, destroy Diane de Poitiers, Countess of Breze.

But there is no historical proof that Francis had done anything of the kind. The historical Saint-Vallier had been one of the followers of a traitor, the High Constable of Bourbon. Although condemned to death, he had been pardoned by the King. But he was a prisoner in the dungeon of Loches, and in no position to interrupt royal cavortings at the Louvre in Paris.

The historical basis of *Le roi s'amuse*, then, is slight. Hugo has used these real historical characters, or at least their names, to symbolize various states and conditions. Francis is lechery and despotism, abuse of absolute power. Triboulet is paternal love co-existing with malevolence, which is itself symbolized by physical deformity. Saint-Vallier is parental dignity and honour ridiculed. Although Hugo scatters throughout his play several verifiable historical facts concerning the minor characters—no doubt in order to help create an authentic period atmosphere, and perhaps in the hope that part of their credibility will rub off upon Francis and Triboulet—the fact remains that *Le roi s'amuse* is not in any sense based on history. It is a romantic melodrama in verse with an underlying message which is republican and anti-royalist. The picture of France during the Renaissance which it presents has no basis in reality, and even the play's theatrical effectiveness relies almost as much on the splendour of its stage settings as it does on Hugo's verse, though the playwright was an excellent craftsman and responsible for several superb *coups de théâtre*. One of these is the scene in Act III in which Triboulet, searching for his daughter in the Royal antichamber at the Louvre, and highly suspicious of the courtiers, dissimulates his anxiety and affects a mood of jesting indifference, only to round on the courtiers in a fury when he realizes that his daughter Blanche is with the King. Another occurs in Act V. Triboulet, after a long soliloquy delivered over the sack which he thinks contains the body of Francis, is about to throw it into the Seine, when suddenly he hears in the distance the voice of the King singing his song about the fickleness of women.

Hugo's play is in five acts, to each of which the author has given a title, which is the name of the character who plays a

LEFT: Victor Hugo's design for Act II of the play (Act I, sc. ii of the opera)

33

prominent role in the act in question. Act I is M. de Saint-Vallier (who in the opera becomes Count Monterone); Act II, Saltabadil (Sparafucile); Act III, the King (The Duke of Mantua); Act IV, Blanche (Gilda); Act V, Triboulet (Rigoletto). Piave and Verdi have of necessity compressed and shortened the text, but they have remained remarkably faithful to the original and have followed the shape, structure and dramatic development of Hugo's play just as closely as they have its dramatic, aesthetic and moral intentions. Their opera is divided into three acts, the first of which is in two scenes. Act I of Hugo corresponds to Act I, scene i of Piave-Verdi; Act II to Act I, scene ii; Act III to Act II; while Hugo's Act IV and Act V are contained within the opera's Act III. The passage of time between the play's fourth and fifth acts—unspecified but not necessarily more than an hour or so—is represented in the opera by a kind of dramatically-musically licensed pause (*see* p. 75).

In general, the reduction of the play to libretto-length has been achieved by the deletion of all historical, local and national allusions which tie the events too closely to France at the time of Francis I, by the omission of a number of very minor characters, and by a severe abridgement of the dialogue. But Piave has retained many of Hugo's best lines and has retained their flavour in translating them into Italian. 'In a drama', Verdi decreed, 'style and language have no value unless accompanied by action', and Piave has served Hugo's drama well in compressing and so speeding up the action of the play. Indeed, the contemporary French novelist and critic Michel Butor wrote (in the *Nouvelle revue française*, in November 1964), apparently without intending any ironical overtone, that '*Il est certain que* Le roi s'amuse *a trouvé sa véritable forme dans* Rigoletto.' ('It is certain that *Le roi s'amuse* has found its real form in *Rigoletto.*')

Piave, Verdi and the Teatro Fenice had, of course, already had a success with an opera based on Victor Hugo seven years earlier, when the French play *Hernani* had become the Italian opera *Ernani*. Piave's compression of the play had been expertly done, and his adaptation of *Le roi s'amuse* in 1850 was even more successful. Apart from altering the locale from Paris in the 1520s to Mantua in roughly the same period, Verdi and Piave followed *Le roi s'amuse* even more closely than they had *Hernani*. They were not allowed by the military censors to include the scene in the play in which Blanche is brought before the King whom she is astonished to find is her young admirer. The King laughs at her plight, offers to make her his official mistress and, when she runs off into another room to escape from him, takes out a key, follows her in and locks the door, the poor girl having chosen to seek sanctuary in, of all places, the King's own bedroom. 'The sheep seeks refuge in the lion's den' is the comment of Marot (the opera's Marullo). With the exception of this scene, however, composer and librettist were extremely faithful to the original.

Having been forced to turn a French King into an Italian Duke, Verdi and Piave may have derived some private amusement by thinking of the character in their own minds not as a sixteenth-century Duke of Mantua but as their own ruler, the depraved Carlo III, who had become Duke of Parma in 1849, following the abdication of his father. Carlo, a young petty tyrant, was to end his life in 1854, stabbed to death in the streets of Parma at the age of thirty. A description of his brief life would make that of *Rigoletto*'s Duke of Mantua sound quite saintly. Verdi's pupil Emanuele Muzio refers to Carlo III in a letter to their mutual benefactor Antonio Barezzi:

A few days ago, our Master was in Milan where he lodged at the Hôtel de la Ville. I saw him one evening at Count Barni's apartment, and he was in an extremely compromising condition. He was so highly-strung, he couldn't stand up! Poor man! My friend assures me that the orgy went on until four in the morning, and then he left for his capital in an open carriage, accompanied by only one person.

Fine people we've been given, by the grace of God!

I myself heard him say he had been slandered, and that it wasn't he who had people beaten, but a police deputy who had been dismissed. Let's hope to God it's true and that all the barbarities committed in this wretched land will cease at last.

In an edition of Piave's libretto of *Rigoletto*, printed for a revival of the opera during the Carnival season of 1852–53 at the Teatro La Fenice, a preface is included which repeats some of the statements made by Victor Hugo in his original preface to the play, but which goes on to indicate certain differences of emphasis between play and opera:

Piave's Rigoletto (Triboulet) is less guilty than the French hunchback; he does not go about *montrant* his master *sans cesse du doigt la femme à seduire, la soeur à enlever, la fille à déshonorer*; Gilda does not become a *fille seduite et perdue*, and Maddalena is less despicable than Maguelonne.

The Duke of Signor Piave is one of those many irresponsible men whom history and the world is full of, and we believe it indeed a very moral purpose to demonstrate what terrible consequences can follow from the wiles and even from the thoughtlessness of a seducer. . . .

We who love *l'art chaste* and not *l'art prude* do not believe we are faithless to our principles in publishing *Rigoletto* . . . in which the most terrible and violent passions are contrasted with their deplorable effects and with the terrible punishment by which they are followed.

The first acts of both play and opera begin with the same dialogue. In the play, the opening lines are those addressed by the King to M. De la Tour-Landry:

The King: Count, I want to bring to a climax this adventure. A plebeian woman, of obscure birth, no doubt, but charming!

In the opera, this becomes:

> Duke: I want to bring to a climax this adventure with my
> unknown plebeian beauty.

And, having begun similarly, play and opera remain close to
each other. The magnificent scene in Hugo's Act II between
Triboulet and the assassin Saltabadil retains its flavour in the
opera, as well as most of its dialogue, though some of
Saltabadil's replies to Triboulet's questions are shortened for
Sparafucile. A comparison of 'Pari siamo', Rigoletto's great
monologue after Sparafucile's exit, with its source in *Le roi
s'amuse*, is revealing both of Piave's fidelity to Hugo, and of his
method of compression and abridgement. Rigoletto's monologue, in Italian and English, will be found on p. 112. Here is
Hugo's original—not the present author's prose translation but
a nineteenth-century English verse translation which, though
not entirely accurate, is suitable for performance. The lines in
brackets do not appear in the opera:

Triboulet:

How much alike his cruel trade to mine;
His sword is sharp, but with a tongue more keen
I stab the heart! Aye, deeper far than he.
The old man cursed me! [even as he spoke
I mocked and taunted him; and yet, oh shame,
My lip but smiled. His sorrow touched my soul.
Accurst indeed!] For man with nature leagues
To make me wicked, heartless and depraved!
Buffoon! Oh heav'n! deformed, despised, disgraced;
[Always that thought, or sleeping or awake,
It haunts my dreams, and tortures me by day:
The vile buffoon, the wretched fool of court]
Who must not, cannot, dare not, for his hire
Do aught but laugh! [Oh grief! Oh misery!
The poorest beggar, or the vilest slave,
The very galley convict in his chains,
May] weep [and soothe his anguish with his tears.]
Alas, I dare not! [Oh, 'tis hard to feel
Bowed down to earth with sore infirmities;

Jealous of beauty, strength or manly grace,
With splendour circled, making me more sad.
In vain my wretchedness would hide from man,
In vain my heart would sob its griefs alone.]
My patron comes, [the joyous laughing king,
Beloved of women! heedless of the tomb;]
Well-shapen, handsome, King of France—and young,
[And with his foot he spurns me as I hide,]
And, yawning, cries, 'Come, make me laugh, buffoon'.
[Alas, poor fool! And yet I am a man,
And rancorous hate, and pride, and baffled rage
Boil in my brain, and make my soul like hell.
Ceaseless I meditate some dark design,
Yet, feeling, nature, thought, must I conceal,
At at my master's sign make sport for all.
Abjection base! where'er I move to feel
My foot encumbered with its galling chain.
By men avoided, loathed and trampled on,
By women treated as a harmless dog.]
Huh! Gallant courtiers and brave gentlemen,
Oh, how I hate you! Here behold your foe.
[Your bitter sneers I pay you back with scorn,
And foil and countermine your proud desires.
Like the bad spirit, in your master's ear
I whisper death to each aspiring aim,
Scattering, with cruel pleasure, leaf by leaf,
The bud of hope—long ere it come to flower.]
You made me wicked: [yet what grief to live
But to drop poison in the cup of joy
That others drink! and if within my breast
One kindly feeling springs, to thrust it forth
And stun reflection with these jingling bells.
Amidst the feast, the dance, the glittering show,
Like a foul demon, seek I to destroy,
For very sport, the happiness of all,
Covering with hollow, false, malignant smile
The venomed hate that festers at my heart.
Yet am I wretched! No, not wretched here!
This door once past, existence comes anew:
Let me forget the world—no past regret
Shall dim the happiness that waits me here.]

> The old man cursed me! Why returns that thought?
> Forbodes it evil? Pshaw! art mad? for shame!

The only important difference between play and opera occurs in the final scene, where Piave and Verdi, by omission, distinctly improve upon Hugo. In the play, a crowd gathers around Triboulet and the corpse of Blanche, and the half-crazed father enacts a scene of distracted grief with the onlookers. A doctor pushes his way through the crowd, examines Blanche, and announces in clinical language: 'She's dead. She has a very deep wound in her left side. The flowing of the blood has caused death by suffocation.' Triboulet swoons, after a cry of '*J'ai tué mon enfant*' ('I have killed my child'), and the curtain falls. But the opera's scene for father and daughter alone, with Rigoletto's final exclamation recalling Monterone's curse both verbally and musically ('*Ah! La maledizione*'), is formally more satisfying, and certainly more in accord with the mood of both play and opera.

Synopsis of the Plot

Set in Mantua in the sixteenth century, the opera is in three acts.

ACT I, SCENE I: A magnificent hall of the Ducal Palace in Mantua. Doors at the back open into other rooms, all of which are splendidly lit. An elegant assembly of courtiers and ladies moves through the rooms, pages come and go, and there is a general air of festivity. From off-stage come the sounds of dance music and occasional laughter. The Duke of Mantua enters with one of his courtiers, Borsa, and strolls through the crowd, talking of the beautiful girl he has been pursuing, incognito, for the past three months. He first saw her, he says, in church, and he has followed her to her home, a small house in a dark, narrow lane, where a mysterious man visits her every evening. At this point in the Duke's narrative, a group of ladies crosses his field of vision, and his attention is diverted from his story of the beautiful commoner. He praises the beauty of the Countess Ceprano, and when Borsa warns him not to let her husband, Count Ceprano, overhear him, the Duke expounds his view that one pretty woman is the same as another. Today this one pleases him, tomorrow that. He dances with the Countess Ceprano, to the annoyance of her husband.

Rigoletto, the hunchbacked court jester, enters and taunts Count Ceprano, implying that the Duke is already enjoying the favours of the Countess. The Duke and the Countess wander off to an adjoining room, and Rigoletto follows them. Another courtier, Marullo, enters to tell the others of his discovery that old Rigoletto has a mistress whom he visits every evening. This occasions great merriment on the part of the courtiers. The Duke and Rigoletto return, and the Duke mutters to his jester that, though the Countess Ceprano is adorable, her husband is in the way. The malevolent Rigoletto banteringly suggests prison, exile or execution for the Count, a remark which that gentleman overhears. All the courtiers, at one time or another,

have suffered from Rigoletto's tongue; so, when Ceprano asks them to meet him later that evening to plan revenge on the hunchback, they readily agree.

Suddenly a voice outside is heard to demand admittance. It is that of Count Monterone who bursts in to confront the Duke who has seduced his daughter. Rigoletto makes fun of the old man, and, when Monterone continues to denounce him, the Duke has him arrested. As Monterone is led off to prison, he curses both Duke and jester. Rigoletto is terrified.

ACT I, SCENE II: The stage is so arranged that one sees both the courtyard of Rigoletto's house and the lane on the other side of its wall. In the courtyard are a large tree and a marble seat. A door in the wall leads into the lane. Above the wall is the balcony of the house, connected with the courtyard by a staircase. On the opposite side of the lane can be seen the outer wall of Ceprano's palace. It is night. Rigoletto, a cloak wrapped around him, comes along the lane, followed by a man who now introduces himself as Sparafucile, a professional assassin, and offers his services to Rigoletto. Sparafucile tells the jester that, outside the town, he keeps an inn, to which his victims are lured

by the charms of his young sister who accosts them in the street. Rigoletto says he has no present need for the assassin's services, but makes a point of asking how he can be found if wanted.

When Sparafucile has departed, Rigoletto soliloquises on the similarity between himself and the assassin. Both are paid to wound, one with his tongue, the other with his sword. He curses the fate that brought him into the world deformed, and expresses his loathing for the Duke's courtiers. He keeps remembering the old man's curse, but, shaking off his disturbed mood, he enters the courtyard of his house and greets his daughter, Gilda. He enjoins upon her that she must never leave the house alone, for he is fearful that she will fall a victim to one of the courtiers. Gilda asks her father why he never mentions their family name, or her mother, and Rigoletto can only reply: 'Ah, don't speak to a miserable man of his lost happiness.' He calls Gilda's nurse, Giovanna, and reminds her that she must watch carefully over his beloved child. Thinking he hears a noise outside, he rushes into the street. As he does so, the Duke slips into the courtyard, noticed only by Giovanna to whom he throws a purse of money, and hides behind the tree. Rigoletto, having assured himself that no one is loitering outside, returns to say goodnight to Gilda. He addresses her as daughter, which surprises the Duke.

When her father has gone, Gilda confesses to Giovanna her remorse at not having confided to him that she has frequently been followed by the handsome young man she saw in church. She murmurs to herself that she loves him and, as she utters the phrase, the Duke steps out from his hiding-place and repeats it. They exchange vows of love, and he tells Gilda his name is Gualtier Maldé, and that he is an impecunious student. Footsteps are heard in the street outside and, fearful that it may be her father returning, Gilda insists that the young man leave. After he has gone, she repeats his name tenderly to herself, sings of her love for him, and goes into the house.

The voices Gilda had heard outside were those of the courtiers who have assembled, all masked, to take their revenge on Rigoletto. The jester returns, and the courtiers persuade him that their intention is to abduct Ceprano's wife from the palace opposite, and take her to the Duke. Rigoletto agrees to help them, and allows them to bandage his eyes under the impression that he is simply donning a mask. He holds the ladder for them as they climb over his own wall, enter his house and carry off Gilda. Finding himself alone, he becomes suspicious and, tearing off the bandage, rushes into his house to find his daughter gone. It is the old man's curse, he exclaims as he falls, swooning, to the ground.

ACT II: A drawing-room in the Ducal Palace. On the walls are full-length portrait paintings of the Duke and his Duchess, and the furniture includes a large chair placed by a velvet-covered table. The Duke enters in a state of agitation: he has returned to Rigoletto's house only to find it deserted. Certain that Gilda has been abducted, he is torn between rage that anyone should dare so to cross him, and pity for the girl who, he says, has awakened for the first time feelings of affection and constancy in his heart.

Marullo, Ceprano, Borsa and the other courtiers now enter and gleefully narrate their adventures of the previous night when, with Rigoletto's unwitting collaboration, they had carried off the girl they believed to be his mistress. Realizing that they must be referring to Gilda, the Duke is delighted when they inform him they have brought her to the palace. He rushes off, intending to console her and tell her that he loves her. A moment later, the grief-stricken Rigoletto enters, attempting to conceal his distress beneath his usual banteringly cynical manner. He looks about him uncertainly for clues as to Gilda's whereabouts, even snatching up a handkerchief from the table in the hope that it may be hers. He asks for the Duke, and is told he is still asleep. But, when a page enters to say that the Duchess wishes to speak to her husband, and the courtiers pretend that he has gone hunting, Rigoletto suddenly realizes the Duke must be with Gilda. The courtiers tell him to look for his mistress somewhere else, but, exclaiming, 'It's my daughter I want', he turns on the astonished but not noticeably abashed assembly, alternately threatening and pleading with them.

Suddenly, Gilda runs into the room and throws herself into her father's arms. Overjoyed that she is safe, Rigoletto is only too willing to believe the escapade was nothing but a harmless joke, until Gilda's tears and obvious shame convince him the matter is more serious. 'Let my blushes be seen by you alone,' Gilda says to him, and her father orders the courtiers to leave them.

When they are alone together, Gilda confesses to Rigoletto that she had been attracted by a young man whom she had seen at church and who followed her home. When she was kidnapped, she was brought to the palace where, she implies, she has just been raped by that same young man, the Duke. As Rigoletto attempts to comfort her, Monterone crosses the room under guard, on his way to prison. He pauses to address the Duke's portrait: 'I have cursed you in vain, oh Duke, for no thunderbolt or sword has struck you down, and you live happily still.' But, as Monterone is led away, Rigoletto calls after him that he is mistaken, and that he will be avenged. He then swears a terrible vengeance on the Duke, while Gilda in vain tries to counsel forgiveness so that they may, in turn, be forgiven by heaven.

ACT III: The curtain rises to reveal Sparafucile's inn, a dilapidated two-storey house outside Mantua, on the right bank of the river Mincio. One can see, on the ground floor, a room that is used for drinking and public entertaining, and a narrow staircase leading to an attic with a bed and an unshuttered balcony. A door in the ground-floor room leads outside to the bank of the river. It is night. Sparafucile sits at a table, polishing

his belt. Outside, watching through a chink in the wall, are Rigoletto and Gilda. Gilda has told her father that she is still in love with the Duke, and that she believes he really returns her love. Rigoletto has brought her here to prove to her that her lover is worthless and inconstant. He tells her to wait and watch, and soon she sees the Duke enter the inn from another door, and hears him order wine and a room for the night. He sings a cynical song about the fickleness of women and the inadvisibility of either trusting or loving them.

Sparafucile brings the Duke a bottle of wine and two glasses, and knocks on the ceiling with his sword, which is a signal for his sister Maddalena to appear. At this signal, a young girl in gipsy dress runs down the stairs and into the room. The Duke rushes to embrace her, but she laughs and skips away from him. While they are engaged in this preliminary sex-play, Sparafucile goes outside to Rigoletto whom he has been expecting, and, taking him aside so that Gilda shall not hear, asks if he has finally decided whether the man is to live or to die. Rigoletto promises to return later and let him know. Sparafucile makes his way behind the house, and Gilda and Rigoletto remain outside while the Duke flirts with Maddalena in the tavern. Gilda,

46

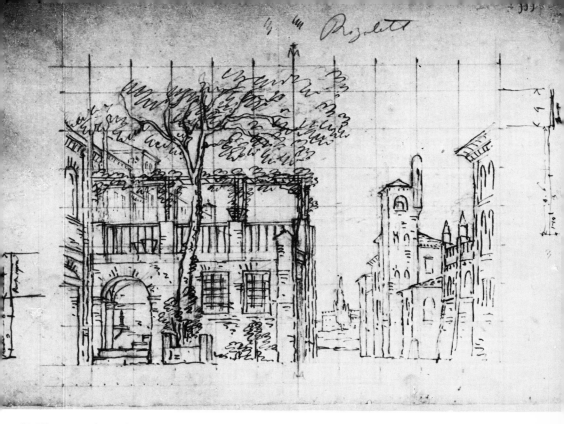

disillusioned and heart-broken, is persuaded by her father to
return home, dress in male attire, and set out on horseback for
Verona, whither her father will follow the next day. When she
pleads with Rigoletto to accompany her now, he says that he
cannot: there is something he still must do.

Gilda leaves, and Rigoletto disappears behind the house,
returning with Sparafucile and counting out money which he
hands over, promising to pay the remainder when the job is
done. It is arranged that he is to return at midnight to collect the
body. Sparafucile casually asks the victim's name, to which
Rigoletto's splendidly extravagant reply is: 'Do you want my
name as well? He is Crime, and I am Punishment.' (This is an
exact translation of Victor Hugo's '*Veux-tu savoir le mien
également?/Il s'appelle le crime, et moi le châtiment.*')

Rigoletto departs, a storm begins to brew, the Duke arranges
to spend the night with Maddalena, and he is shown up to his
room. Attracted by the handsome young stranger, Maddalena
remains below with her brother whom she attempts to dissuade
from murdering the young man. But Sparafucile does not
understand this sentiment: after all, the sum of twenty crowns is
at stake. 'Why not kill the old hunchback instead, and still take

the money?' Maddalena suggests, thus offending her brother's sense of professional etiquette. One does not murder one's own clients, Sparafucile points out coldly.

At this moment, Gilda reappears outside, dressed in male riding clothes. She approaches the inn, and overhears brother and sister arguing over which of the two shall die, her lover or her father. Sparafucile offers his sister a compromise: if, before Rigoletto's expected return at midnight, another stranger should chance to call at the inn, he will be murdered instead. Otherwise, Maddalena's handsome young man must die. Maddalena fears that, so late on such a stormy night, no one is likely to arrive. She weeps, and Gilda, touched by the girl's pity for the Duke, resolves to give her own life for him. Summoning up all her courage, she knocks at the door, calling: 'Have pity on a beggar who seeks shelter for the night.' Sparafucile takes his dagger and stands behind the door, which Maddalena opens after having extinguished the light. In the darkness Gilda screams 'God forgive them', and then all is silent.

A few moments later, Rigoletto returns. The violence of the

storm lessens, midnight strikes, and Sparafucile emerges from
the inn dragging a sack which, he says, contains the dead body
Rigoletto has asked for. He offers to throw it into the river, but
the hunchback prefers to give himself that satisfaction.
Sparafucile returns inside. As Rigoletto is about to push the
sack into the water, he hears in the distance the Duke's voice
singing his song about the fickleness of women. Amazed and
terrified, Rigoletto opens the sack, and a flash of lightning
clearly reveals the face of his daughter. She is still alive, but she
dies in his arms, asking for his blessing. Rigoletto remembers
Monterone. 'Ah, the curse', he cries in desperation as he falls
across Gilda's lifeless body.

The Music

Verdi sometimes composed full-scale Overtures to his operas, and sometimes not. Often, he set the mood with a brief Prelude, and then took the curtain up without a pause. This is how *Rigoletto* begins (*Preludio ed Introduzione*). The short, ominous Prelude, a mere thirty-five bars, is based on a phrase heard right at the outset on trumpets and trombones, a phrase which, in the opera, is associated with Rigoletto's recollection of Monterone's curse ('*Quel vecchio maledivami*'). The tempo of the Prelude, a mere thirty-five bars, is based on a phrase heard right increases until a climax of forceful chords is reached, punctuated by sinister rumblings on the timpani. The curtain rises quickly, as the fateful chords of the Prelude give way to the festive music of the opening scene played by an off-stage band.

The *banda* was an important element in earlier nineteenth-century Italian opera, usually a brass section used on stage behind the scenes to provide music when the stage picture obviously required the sound to come from somewhere other than the orchestra pit: for dancing, ceremonial processions and the like. Verdi made frequent use of the *banda*, though less so in his later operas. His stage music here, at the beginning of *Rigoletto*, has a splendidly rustic 'Busseto town band' quality which seems ideally suited to the quality of life in a provincial Italian court in the sixteenth century, or at any rate suited to the mythical Mantua in which the events of the opera take place. The joyous dance tunes set the festive mood, and continue under the dialogue of Borsa and the Duke of Mantua, both tenor voices. As we approach the Duke's *ballata* (or ballad), '*Questa o quella*', the violins, flute and oboe of the orchestra proper discreetly replace the *banda* in accompanying the dialogue. '*Questa o quella*' emerges naturally and informally from its surroundings, and merges as easily into the formal dance which follows it. Verdi is concerned, in this opera, not with

LEFT: *A page of the
libretto written by
Piave. Act I, sc. i*

Atto Primo

Grandiosa galleria nel palazzo di Vendome splendidamente
illuminata. Sonvi porte laterali e folla di Cavalieri e Dame.
S'ode dall'interno la musica delle danze. La festa è più
finire.

Scena I
Vendome e Prouvcy dal fondo.

Ve. Della mia bella incognita borghese
Toccare il fin dell'avventura io voglio.

Pu. Di colei che nomar v'odo sì spesso?
Ve. E da tre lune io veggo...

Pu. La sua dimora?
Ve. Di Chatsy nel calle;
Misterioso un uom v'entra ogninotte.

Pu. E sa chi sia l'amante pro?
Ve. Lo ignora.

(Un gruppo di Dame e Cav. attraversen la sala.)

Pu. Quante bellà!... mirate...
Ve. Le vince tutte di Cralatif la sposa.

Pu. Non v'oda il conte, o Duca... (piano)
Ve. A me che importa?

Pu. Dirlo ad altra ei potria...
Ve. Nè sventura per me certo savia.

Diana o Agnese per me pari sono
A quant'altre d'intorno mi vedo;
Del mio core l'impero non cedo
Meglio ad una che ad altra beltà.
La costoro avvenenza è qual dono
Di che il fato ne infiora la vita;
S'oggi questa mi torna gradita,
Forse un'altra doman lo sarà.
La costanza tiranna del core
Detestiamo qual morbo crudele.
Sol chi vuole si serbi fedele,
Non v'è amor, se non v'ha varietà

51

ABOVE: *Carl Ebert
(right, with book in
hand) rehearsing his
production of* Rigoletto
*for the New London
Opera Company, at
the Cambridge
Theatre, 1947*

applause-catching high notes, but with characterization. Most
of the high notes one hears in the music of the Duke, Gilda and
Rigoletto are singers' interpolations not to be found in the score
of the opera. The rakish 6/8 rhythm of '*Questa o quella*' is
enchanting, a forerunner of 1920s swing, and the *ballata* must be
sung with lightness and elegance. Indeed, this observation
applies to all of the Duke's music. One has hardly realized that
'*Questa o quella*' has come to an end when the rhythm and tempo
change to that of the more proper and stately minuet, and it is
above this imitation, though probably an unconscious one, of
the minuet in Mozart's *Don Giovanni* that the Duke flirts
gracefully and banteringly with the Countess Ceprano ('*Partite?
Crudele!*'), to the accompaniment of a stage band of strings.

Rigoletto now makes his entrance, while the first stage band
repeats some of the melodies already heard. A few of the guests
now dance a *perigordino* or *périgourdine*, a lively French country
dance in 6/8 time, whose name comes from Périgord. An
appropriate dance, Verdi must have felt, for the court of Francis
I. He may have written the music with this in mind, and allowed
the French dance to remain when the locale of the opera was

changed to Italy. The *banda* music of the beginning of the scene now returns briefly at the entrance of Marullo, and the gay chorus in which Marullo arouses the interest of the other courtiers in plotting against Rigoletto fits easily, together with the dialogue of the Duke and Rigoletto, into the festive dance rhythms which still predominate throughout this ensemble, with the pit orchestra and the stage band now ingeniously combined.

The joyous atmosphere is dissipated by the entrance of Monterone whose part is nowadays more often than not sung by a bass, although Verdi stipulated a baritone voice. After Monterone has declaimed his accusation against the Duke, Rigoletto mocks the old man who then pronounces a curse on both Duke and jester. Rigoletto's ariso, mocking the outraged father, is accompanied and punctuated by orchestral figures which vividly illustrate the evil, destructive side of the hunchback's nature, and the curse uttered by Monterone is, in context, as chilling as the music of the Commendatore's statue in *Don Giovanni*. The scene ends with an ensemble which begins in hushed dismay with the voices of the Duke and the courtiers

ABOVE: *Gian-Piero Mastromei as Rigoletto. Royal Opera House, Covent Garden, 1976*

53

ABOVE: *Geraint Evans as Rigoletto in Zeffirelli's Covent Garden production, 1964. Sir Geraint sang his first and only performance of the role on the first night of this production*

OPPOSITE: *Lawrence Tibbett (1896–1960), leading baritone of the Metropolitan Opera in the thirties and forties, as Rigoletto*

in unison, and works its way up to a vigorous conclusion. It is at the very end that some conductors make an absurd cut of seven or eight bars: presumably this is an act of criticism of what they take to be Verdi's over-emphatic writing, for the time saved is to be measured in seconds! In this short opening scene, which takes about a quarter of an hour to perform, the plot of the drama has been set forth and even considerably advanced. The old Italian opera would, by now, have got no further than overture, opening chorus, and aria revealing the hero or heroine's state of mind. It is not surprising that Verdi was accused of succumbing to German influences in *Rigoletto*. But the influence to which he succumbed, the Austro-Germanic symphonic tradition of Haydn, Mozart and Beethoven, had been apparent in Verdi's first opera, *Oberto*, written a good twelve years before *Rigoletto*.

The second scene of Act I opens with the duet between Rigoletto and the assassin Sparafucile, a beautifully atmospheric piece of writing which sets the scene more vividly with its use of clarinet, bassoon and lower strings than any scenic designer could do. Rigoletto enters, and we hear for the first time his disturbed recollection of Monterone's curse, '*Quel vecchio maledivami*'. He is accosted by Sparafucile, and here

ABOVE: *Sherrill
Milnes (Rigoletto)
and Placido Domingo
(Duke), at the
Metropolitan Opera,
New York, 1977*

Verdi's use of the orchestra is masterly, as is his decision to give the gloomy and sinister melody of the duet not to the voices but to cello and double bass, with a taut rhythmic accompaniment of other instruments. The two voices which converse freely over the melody are dark of timbre (baritone and bass), as are the instruments: solo cello and double-bass, both muted, with their accompanying clarinets, bassoons, violas, cellos and double-basses. The voices of the two men are never heard together in real duet, but only in the exchange of their dialogue. Sparafucile makes his exit singing a sustained low F, as he repeats his name to Rigoletto. In the course of the duet he has mentioned that he comes from Burgundy, thus revealing the original French provenance of the plot. Piave ought really to have noticed this and altered 'Borgognone' (Bugundian) to, say, 'Bolognese'. (In *Le roi s'amuse*, the assassin Saltabadil admits to Triboulet that he is a gipsy and from Burgundy.) Admittedly, Rigoletto suspects that Sparafucile is a stranger or foreigner— '*Straniero*?' he asks, sharply—but this merely means 'not of the immediate vicinity'. A Mantuan would certainly have considered someone from Venice, Parma or Bologna to be a foreigner.

56

Rigoletto's great soliloquy, 'Pari siamo', part recitative and part arioso, which is a kind of half-way house beween recitative and melody, is a superb example of Verdi's extraordinary ability to harness his psychological insight to his melodic genius. Rigoletto compares himself with Sparafucile. 'We are alike', he exclaims. 'I have my tongue, he has his dagger. I am a man who laughs, and he one who slays.' 'Pari siamo' is not an aria in the old style, in fact it is not an aria at all, for it contains nothing which one could call a tune, although phrase after phrase is searingly memorable. It is, rather, the operatic equivalent, in form and in stature, of a great Shakespearian soliloquy. Verdi gives it the variety of pace of a spoken monologue with the six changes of tempo which he calls for during its performance. It begins slowly and broodingly, marked *adagio*: the first change is to *allegro* when Rigoletto rails against nature for having made him deformed, then back to *adagio* as he bemoans his inability to weep, next to a *moderato* as he considers his young master, and to *allegro* to express his hatred of the courtiers. An *andante* passage speaks of his domestic life, and this quickens first to *allegro* and then to *allegro*

BELOW: *Alfredo Kraus as the Duke of Mantua, at the old Metropolitan Opera House, 1966*

ABOVE: *Stafford Dean (Sparafucile), Gillian Knight (Maddalena) and Jon Andrew (Duke) at Sadler's Wells Theatre, London, 1967*

vivo as he shakes off his forebodings and enters the house to greet his daughter. The high G at the end of the monologue, on '*è follia*', which every baritone interpolates in performance, is a lower E in Verdi's score, but it would be too much to expect any self-respecting Rigoletto to forego showing off the top of his voice at this point.

At the quickening of the tempo to *allegro vivo*, and the brightening of the key to C major, without a break in the music the soliloquy becomes a duet, as Gilda comes out of the house to meet her father. Their extended duet is one of the finest in a long series of duets in which Verdi explored the father-daughter relationship, through a number of operas beginning with his very first, *Oberto*, in 1839. It is surely not entirely by accident that he found himself writing so frequently for baritone or bass fathers and soprano daughters or daughter-surrogates. Verdi had lost his own children soon after they were born; his relationship with his parents was the uneasy and embarrassed

LEFT: *Scene from Walter Felsenstein's production of* Rigoletto, *Staatsoper, Hamburg, 1962. Arturo Sergi as the Duke of Mantua*

one of a child who has moved out of his parents' social and intellectual class into a world they cannot share; and his sister had died of meningitis in her teens. Perhaps the lack of close family relationships of this kind in his real life led Verdi to create them on the stage.

The long, free-ranging duet between Rigoletto and Gilda encompasses a variety of moods, all of them sketched economically yet clearly, in themes of melodic beauty. The opening allegro of the duet ('*Figlia! Mio padre!*') is sunny and untroubled, and the young Gilda, who one should remember is only sixteen, is presented as an innocent, happy child. But, once past the first joy of greeting, Gilda begins to question her father: the *andante* section for Rigoletto alone ('*Deh non parlare al misero*') is led into by a few *adagio* bars of recitative, but Verdi's recitative, as we have seen, can be as highly charged as the most emotive melody, and the phrase with which Gilda offers to retract her questions is oddly moving. '*Deh non parlare*

al misero', in which Rigoletto remembers his dead wife, is both
expressive and consoling, and the two voices combine in the
final part of the *andante*. An *allegro* follows, containing
Rigoletto's moving, yet broad and expansive phrases as he
replies to Gilda's question about family, friends and country
('*Culta, famiglia, la patria* . . .'). A transitional section, which
contains a brief exchange between Rigoletto and Gilda's old
nurse, Giovanna, leads into the final section of the duet ('*Veglia,
o donna*') whose *moderato* is broken into for the surreptitious
entrance of the Duke into the garden, but is resumed again at
the reprise of '*Veglia, o donna*'. The demands of the drama are all-
important, and are kept firmly in mind by Verdi. A first attempt
at a reprise of '*Veglia, o donna*' is broken off in mid-phrase so that
the suspicious Rigoletto may investigate a noise in the street.
Frequently, in stage performance, one encounters an especially
disfiguring and insensitive cut here, for some conductors break
off the melody at its first hearing. The reprise, when it comes, is
for Rigoletto and for Gilda who decorates the vocal line her
father sings. It is important musically, therefore, that the
melody shall have been heard complete as a solo, first sung by

LEFT: *Richard Tucker (1914–75) as the Duke of Mantua, a role he sang frequently at the Metropolitan Opera, as did his brother-in-law, Jan Peerce*

baritone and then soprano; it is equally important dramatically that the shaping of the scene as a piece of music-drama not be tampered with.

The *arioso* which introduces the duet, '*È il sol dell' anima*' is as melodically charged as is virtually every bar of this opera. The descending phrase ('*No, chè troppo è bello*'), in which Gilda confesses she is attracted by the unknown stranger whom she met in church, is one which we are to meet again in a later Verdi opera, *La traviata*, where it becomes Violetta's great cry, '*Amami, Alfredo*'. The phrase is almost a Verdian trademark, for it had already made appearances in *Il corsaro* (1848) and *La battaglia di Legnano* (1849) before its use in *Rigoletto*. Although Verdi was almost certainly not consciously aware of the fact, the phrase first occurs in Donizetti's *Pia de' Tolomei*, to the words '*Pia mendace*'. Donizetti's opera was produced in Venice in 1837. Giuseppina Strepponi, Verdi's mistress, sang Pia in Rome in 1838, and in Milan in the spring of 1839 at which time Verdi probably heard the opera.

The duet, '*È il sol dell' anima*', especially the Duke's elegantly insincere solo beginning, is exquisite. The voices of Borsa and

OVERLEAF: *Set for Act I, sc. i of the first Metropolitan Opera production of* Rigoletto, *1883*

61

Ceprano are heard assembling in the street outside, which brings from Giovanna a warning which is considerably briefer than that which Brangaene utters to Tristan and Isolde in another time and place and opera. The lovers say farewell in a short concluding *allegro* which, if fairly conventional, is nonetheless effective. The entire duet is enhanced by Verdi's strikingly original, and in this instance also strikingly simple instrumentation: high violins and violas, playing as lightly and softly as possible. Sopranos and tenors appear to find it difficult to resist the temptation to sing their final '*addio*' on the high D flat, an octave above the note written by the composer.

Gilda begins her recitative and aria, '*Caro nome*' by repeating '*Gualtier Maldè*', the false name the Duke has given her, a name, she says, which is now engraved on her enamoured heart. The aria itself has an artless simplicity which has endeared it to generations of audiences and performers. Some English-language critics have found difficulty in accepting passages of coloratura from the supposedly simple and ingenuous Gilda, but surely this is to carry Anglo-Saxon distrust of the baroque too far. Gilda's *fioriture*, or ornamental figures, are always dramatically or emotionally significant, and are never used for purposes of aimless display. This E major aria is

BELOW: *Set for Act III of the first Metropolitan Opera production of* Rigoletto, *1883*

not the virtuoso piece which some sopranos try to turn it into. The singer should always bear in mind Verdi's comments on it in his letter to Carlo Borsi (*see* p. 87). '*Caro nome*' is not only a most beautiful piece of music from its opening woodwind introduction to Gilda's final trill, but is also completely in character, though its beauty and its psychological rightness can sometimes be obscured in performances by *prime donne* who insist on interpolating high notes, and altering the ending in order to do so. It is foolish to be puritanical about the sheer physical thrill of the high note: certain Bellini and Donizetti arias, and some by Verdi, are positively enhanced by the singer's insertion of a note unthought of by the composer, and it is also a legitimate pleasure to hear the second stanza of a *cabaletta*, or fast concluding section of an aria, decorated. But '*Caro nome*' is not music of this kind. Like several of Verdi's most memorable tunes, it grows from a simple scale, in this case descending from E to F sharp. This delicate aria must be sung as written, to achieve its proper effect, with the ending, a long diminuendo trill on E, sung off-stage as Verdi intended, while the courtiers are gathering outside in the street, the male voices bringing a touch of menace to Gilda's idyllic reverie. The entire aria has a unique quality of virginal young love, trust and innocence, and this is emphasized by the delicacy and imagination of the orchestration, from the solo violin figures which punctuate Gilda's confession of love, to the warning tremolo which accompanies the last reprise of the melody.

The finale to the act is unconventional in that it brings the curtain down, not on a huge ensemble, but on the solitary figure of Rigoletto. The abduction scene, with Rigoletto unwittingly helping the courtiers, is fine, though the chorus, '*Zitti, zitti*', has by now come to sound to our ears like the hackneyed prototype of all conspiratorial choruses. It is our ears which are hackneyed, however, and not Verdi's music. At first hearing it must have been riotously effective. After the courtiers have carried her off, Gilda's voice is heard from a distance, Rigoletto realizes he has been tricked, and he recalls once again Monterone's curse as the curtain falls to emphatic chords from an orchestra now brought to a high pitch of excitement.

Act II begins with the Duke's recitative, '*Ella mi fu rapita*', and aria, '*Parmi veder le lagrime*'. At this point in the play, the courtiers inform the King that they have abducted Triboulet's

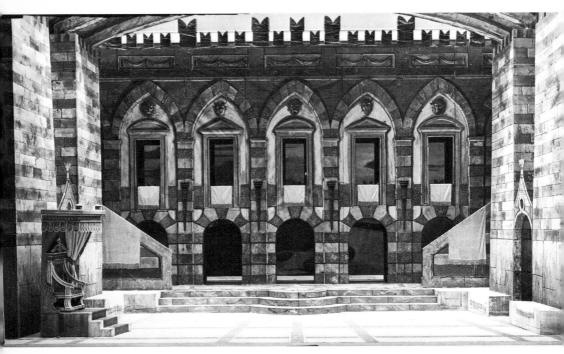

*Designs by Eugene
Berman for a
production at the
Metropolitan Opera,
New York, 1951.*
ABOVE: *Act I, sc. i.*
OPPOSITE: *Act III*

wife or mistress, and they produce Blanche. The King is
delighted, Blanche is distressed and terrified, and the scene in
which she is forced to take unsuccessful refuge in the King's
own bedchamber ensues. Forbidden to include this scene in
their opera, Verdi and Piave substituted a dramatically
conventional recitative, aria and cabaletta for the Duke. In the
recitative he describes how he returned to Rigoletto's house
only to find it deserted. In the aria, he laments the loss of Gilda
whom he thinks he could have loved with a sincerity and
constancy hitherto notably lacking in his temperament. The aria
is a charming and graceful *andante* in the style of the old *bel canto*
operas. In giving the heartless young rake music of such
heartfelt sincerity, Verdi might be thought here to have
momentarily lost his grasp of the character. Perhaps because
Piave's words do not give any indication of whether or not the
Duke is at this moment sincere, or at any rate deluded into
thinking himself sincere, Verdi's music could as easily be sung
by one of his earlier tenor heroes. But this tenor is more of an
anti-hero, like two of Verdi's earlier tenor characters, Corrado
in *Il corsaro* and Carlo in *I masnadieri*. Still it is possible to take the

66

view that '*Parmi veder le lagrime*' is psychologically accurate, and that the Duke can indulge these sentimental feelings about Gilda precisely because he thinks he has lost her. It is true that when he finds her again a few moments later, he will revert to type. Whichever view one takes, it would surely be churlish to regret the existence of so lovely a tenor aria. Its preceding recitative broadens, at the words '*colei che prima potè in questo core . . .*', into music of melodic splendour that few other composers would squander in the recitative preceding an aria. One further note: at the climax of the aria, on the first syllable of the word '*angeli*', the high note in Verdi's score is the tenor's G flat above the stave, but the note one invariably hears in performance is the higher B flat.

The courtiers now recount their adventure of the previous night in a lively and tuneful chorus with amusing and effective juxtaposition of *fortissimo* and *pianissimo*, and the Duke reacts in a cabaletta, '*Possente amor*', on which the musical commentators pour scorn and which is frequently omitted from stage performance. But it is by no means a despicable piece, and deserves to be heard. In any case, one does not improve the reading of a Shakespeare sonnet by omitting the less good lines, and the omission of '*Possente amor*' leaves a musically ungrammatical gap, ugly even to musically untutored ears, between the half-close at the Duke's last words ('*Ah, tutto il ciel non mi rapi*') and the music which herald's Rigoletto's entrance.

Rigoletto's scene with the courtiers is one of the most effective and affecting in the opera. The form is that of aria/transitional passage/cabaletta, but completely transmogrified by Verdi. Instead of the aria, there is the ostensibly free form of the first part of the scene, Rigoletto's exchange of dialogue with Marullo and the other courtiers, the studied indifference of his clown's song, '*la ra, la ra*', and the *de haut en bas* scorn of the courtiers. Throughout the scene, the action is being continually

RIGHT: *Gianna D'Angelo (Gilda) and Ettore Bastianini (Rigoletto) at the Chicago Lyric Opera in 1962*

advanced. Rigoletto desperately searches for a clue to Gilda's whereabouts, the Duke's page comes in to summon his master to the Duchess, Rigoletto realizes Gilda is with the Duke, the courtiers tell him to look elsewhere for his mistress, and he replies with his proud, pathetic cry, '*Io vo' mia figlia*' ('It's my daughter I want'). The music closely follows the course of the drama, with its changes of rhythm, tempo and key. The anger of '*Cortigiani, vil' razza dannata*', the cabaletta equivalent, is expressed in a steady *andante* tempo for the voice, supported by an agitated accompaniment which gives movement and pulse to Rigoletto's tremendous outburst of fury. The second section of '*Cortigiani*', with its cello obbligato as Rigoletto makes a pathetic attempt to gain Marullo's sympathy, is extremely moving. Marullo, Rigoletto says, has always been kinder to him than the others. Surely he will have pity now. (Marullo, in Hugo's play, was not just another courtier but Maître Clement Marot, the Court Poet, and no nobleman. There is no love lost between him and Triboulet, but they are both entertainers in the employ of the King, and Triboulet at this point in the play hopes to appeal to a fellow feeling. Although he hurls abuse at the noblemen—'*Courtisans! Courtisans! démons! race damnée!*' etc—he addresses Marot in different terms, reminding him that under his court livery there beats the heart of a man of the people: '*Un coeur d'homme du peuple, encor, sous ta livrée*'.)

The audience may be moved by Rigoletto's plea for pity, can hardly fail to be, but not the courtiers, not even Marullo. The sudden entry of Gilda, and Rigoletto's realization that his daughter has been raped by the Duke, are made doubly effective if the director remembers, and reminds his performers, that this is also the first time Gilda has seen her father dressed as a jester. She has never known his profession. She discovers his shame at the same moment as he discovers hers. Rigoletto finds a new dignity as he dismisses the courtiers in a passage of recitative, most of it on the one note, C, and the courtiers make their exit with an eight-bar sotto voice chorus.

The act ends with what the score describes simply as scene and duet. It is really a full-scale finale, miniature only in the sense that it is carried by two voices alone. Six bars of recitative lead into Gilda's solo, '*Tutte le feste al tempio*' which is virtually a complete aria. The girl's essential innocence is touchingly conveyed, the highly expressive opening bars for solo oboe

setting a tone of elegiac melancholy which becomes more impassioned as the aria proceeds. Rigoletto's reply, '*Solo per me l'infamia*', displays a pathetic dignity: each of these numbers merges into the next with the minimum of formal gesture. The duet proper, which begins with Rigoletto's '*Piangi, fanciulla*', is most affecting, Gilda's disjointed, tearful phrases contrasting with Rigoletto's legato, with the violins playing a figure of great consolation. As so often, Verdi's genius produces music of heart-rending beauty by the simplest and most economic of means.

Monterone now appears, on his way to prison, and his bitter address to the Duke's portrait provides a transition to the final, *allegro* section of the duet, '*Sì vendetta, tremenda vendetta*', launched by Rigoletto with the words, '*No, vecchio, t'inganni, un vindice avrai*' ('No, old man, you are mistaken, you shall have an avenger'). Rigoletto sings his song of revenge, and then, to words of urgent restraint, Gilda takes it up. The tempo quickens as the two voices are heard together, and the pulsating accompaniment underlines the drama. The act ends in a flurry of excitement, Rigoletto's determination sweeping aside Gilda's pleas. Conductors usually find they have to wait while Gilda interpolates a penultimate high note and Rigoletto a final one, the vanity of singers being strong enough to override all dramatic and musical considerations!

Act III is superb from its first note to its last. Though it contains a song for the Duke, a quartet, a trio and a final duet, none of these numbers can easily be extracted from its context, not even the famous or infamous 'La donna è mobile', without doing damage to them. The entire act is an arioso of genius, rising at climactic moments to peaks of melody in aria, duet, trio, quartet, but never losing its essential unity, its sense of forward movement, or the sheer perfection of its musical structure.

'La donna è mobile' is part of the opening 'Preludio, scena e canzone'. The Prelude is a mere nine bars of brooding adagio, just enough to set the mood as the curtain rises on the divided scene of inn and river bank to reveal Gilda and her father outside, and Sparafucile inside the tavern, polishing his sword-belt. After several bars of musical dialogue, the Duke, who has entered the inn and ordered wine, breaks into his song. It is said that Verdi did not give his tenor the music of 'La donna è mobile' until the last possible moment. If this is true, it was wise of him, for 'La donna è mobile' is a vulgar, catchy tune and Verdi would not have wanted its effect vitiated in advance of the première. It is also precisely the right kind of tune for this character to sing in this context, and to complain of it in terms of pure music is simply to misunderstand the art of opera. The tune is still in character, and immediately identifiable as it needs to be, when it is used again at the end of the opera, at the moment when Rigoletto thinks he has the Duke's body in a sack. Its words—

OPPOSITE: *Jan Peerce as the Duke, a role he sang at the Metropolitan Opera in the forties and fifties*

La donna è mobile
Qual piume al vento,
Muta d'accento
E di pensiero

—are a reasonably faithful translation of the words sung by the King in Victor Hugo's play:

Souvent femme varie,
Bien fol qui s'y fie!
Une femme souvent
N'est qu'une plume au vent!

(Women are frequently fickle: he who trusts them is foolish. A woman is often like a feather in the wind.)

*Franco Zeffirelli's
production of the opera
at Covent Garden, first
seen in 1964. Decor by
Lila De Nobili.*
ABOVE: *Act I, sc. i.*
OPPOSITE: *Act II*

'*Souvent femme varie*' was a famous dictum of the historical Francis I. Hugo had merely expanded the sentiment into a song.

Verdi ends '*La donna è mobile*', not on the high B so beloved by most exponents of the role, but an octave lower. If the Duke's song is a stroke of genius, so too is the equally famous quartet, in which the Duke, Maddalena, Gilda and Rigoletto voice their widely differing feelings in themes which, each individually suitable, blend into a harmonious and very beautiful whole. This quartet is one of the highlights not only of *Rigoletto* but of all Italian opera. It begins (*allegro:* '*Un dì se ben rammentomi*') as dialogue above a remarkable melodic accompaniment, but it is the second section (*andante:* '*Bella figlia dell' amore*') which is so widely known to millions who have never seen a performance of *Rigoletto*. The melody is first stated by the Duke alone, the other characters entering in a contrasting section, while all four take part in the reprise of the melody. The four voice parts, individual not only in melody but also in the type of emotion expressed, add up to a quartet which is astonishing in its psychological complexity and sheer musical persuasiveness. This is the kind of thing which (as even Victor Hugo realized: *see* p. 25) opera is uniquely equipped to do, and no opera composer has done it more magnificently than Verdi. Sopranos

74

are apt to alter the composer's vocal line to end their part in the
quartet an octave higher than written. To put it mildly, Verdi's
more sensitive, less sensational ending is to be preferred.

The 'Scene following the Quartet' contains musical dialogue
of rich variety. As the storm brews, we first hear graphic
phrases on flute and piccolo, representing lightning. With a
stroke of genius, Verdi uses the humming of an off-stage chorus
to represent the sound of the wind, thus anticipating Debussy
by half a century. The opening phrase of '*Bella figlia dell' amore*' is
heard twice on the clarinet, first to draw attention to the Duke
and Maddalena, then to precede Maddalena's musing on the
young Duke's attractiveness. The Duke, half asleep, repeats his
'*la donna è mobile*', a clarinet taking over the phrases as he
drowsily abandons them.

The storm breaks in the Trio, its closer rumblings first
indicated under the preceding dialogue by cellos, basses and
bass drum, and only dies away at the end of the Trio as Gilda
enters the inn to be murdered. The 'Scene following the Trio'
should follow only after a pause of several seconds, although
this is not indicated in either the score or the libretto, for
somehow at this point the passage of time must be conveyed. In
Le roi s'amuse, the curtain falls here on Act IV, and the

OPPOSITE: *Joan Sutherland (Gilda) and Otakar Kraus (Rigoletto) at Covent Garden, 1957*
LEFT: Rigoletto *in Japan. Yoshinobu Kuribayashi (Rigoletto) and Kyoshi Igarashi (Duke) with other members of the Fujiwaro Opera Company, Tokyo, 1968*

following scene is, in fact, the play's Act V. The opera makes no formal break here, but we are to understand that when Rigoletto enters it is some time later, nearly midnight. The clock strikes midnight—six strokes only are indicated, as church clocks in nineteenth-century Italy apparently never chimed more than six—and Rigoletto takes delivery of the sack from Sparafucile. His '*Quest' è un buffone, ed un potente è questo*' ("This', indicating himself, 'is a buffoon, and this', indicating the sack, 'a man of power') is really the climax of the opera, as it is of Rigoletto's revenge. The repetition of the tenor's '*La donna è mobile*', just as the hunchback is about to throw the sack into the river, is another masterstroke, the cynical indifference of the tune underlining the tragedy. Again, this is operatic writing at its finest, real theatre music as opposed to the concert-in-costume of a great many pre-Verdian Italian operas. The perverse and pathetic joy of Rigoletto's '*Quest' è un buffone . . .*', deflated by the offstage sound of the Duke's song, is now turned to an even more pathetic despair by his discovery that the sack contains the body of his mortally wounded daughter. The opera ends with the simple beauty of the duet for Rigoletto and Gilda '*V'ho ingannato*', whose second section, '*Lassù in cielo*', brings a momentary serenity to Rigoletto's despair as Gilda sings of her vision of heaven. She dies, Rigoletto and the orchestra both recall Monterone's curse, and the curtain falls.

Rigoletto is undoubtedly one of Verdi's masterpieces: even those critics who would consign most of his pre-*Rigoletto* works to oblivion are agreed on this. It also marks the beginning of the composer's second or middle period. Verdi was in no sense a conscious innovator; or, if he was conscious of the significance for Italian opera of what he was doing, he chose not to draw attention to the fact. Unlike many *avant garde* (*soi-disant*) artists of our own age whose creative work seems hardly more than an unnecessary adjunct to their theorizing, Verdi was content to leave theoretical justification to others. He was merely a creator. In *Rigoletto* he continued the process he had begun in the last act of *Luisa Miller* (1849), a move towards opening the closed forms of nineteenth-century Italian opera. He still continued to write his operas in separate numbers, but with so flexible an approach that, as with Wagner, it is not always easy to tell where one number ends or the next begins. Now completely confident of his gifts, Verdi moves with arrogant ease from number to number, linking them not by the jerky recitative and contrived situations of the past, but in whatever way he chooses. Sometimes his most startling inventions will occur in what used to be the no-man's-land between the end of an aria and the beginning of an ensemble. Sometimes, as in *Rigoletto*, he will almost completely by-pass the aria and conceive the work as a series of duets.

The first three operas of Verdi's middle period—*Rigoletto*, *La traviata* and *Il trovatore*—are, as the popular guides to opera point out, 'treasure houses of glorious melody', but they are something more than that: they are a practical demonstration of Verdi's complete escape from subservience to the formal patterns usually accepted by the older composers. Where he continued to find these forms useful, Verdi employed them: but he had, by now, won through to an ability to use, to create, form, rather than be used by it.

In *Rigoletto*, Verdi's working unit is no longer the aria, but the scene. The backbone of the opera is the series of duets between Rigoletto and Gilda, Rigoletto and Sparafucile, Gilda and the Duke, but the formal unit is the scene. The length and position of *Rigoletto*'s arias, duets, recitative dialogue and choruses depend on the structure of the entire scene, whereas in the past the scene had merely been the total of the independent units of aria, recitative, cabaletta and ensemble contained within it. To emphasize the technical innovation in *Rigoletto*, however, is to do the opera an injustice. What is most remarkable about the work is its sustained level of inspiration. As in its companion operas—*La traviata* and *Il trovatore*—an uncanny psychological acumen is allied with a wonderfully spontaneous outpouring of melody, a gift Verdi shared only with Mozart and Schubert.

A use of the orchestra as appropriate and frequently as skilful as that of Berlioz; brilliant delineation of the minor characters, in particular Sparafucile, Maddalena and Monterone; a prodigality of melodic invention; a great advance towards integral structure; remarkable insight into character motivation: these are a few of the attributes which combine to make *Rigoletto* one of the most popular of operas, as well as musically and dramatically one of the finest. A resilient work, it triumphantly survives non-production, bad production, and the vain foibles of musically illiterate singers. Conversely, what superb opportunities it offers to the intelligent interpreter of the role of Rigoletto, so memorably 'burnt into music by Verdi' as Bernard Shaw described it.

The role, indeed the entire opera, is infused with a humanity which puts one in mind of Mozart. In a very real sense, beneath the obvious surface differences, *Rigoletto* is Mozartean. It may appear to be moving towards a quasi-Wagnerian endless melody, but its roots are in the organically developing ensembles of *Don Giovanni* and *Le nozze di Figaro*. From *Rigoletto* onwards, each Verdi opera acquires a strong individual flavour. Arias and duets from his earliest works, from *Oberto, I Lombardi* and *La battaglia di Legnano* could perhaps be interchanged, just as they could in several operas of Rossini, Donizetti and Bellini. But there is no possibility of mistaking pages of *Rigoletto, La traviata* or *Il trovatore* for one another. Each has its distinctive orchestral colouring, its melodic shape and its overall dramatic form. It was the earliest of these three operas, *Rigoletto*, which impelled Rossini to remark that at last he could recognize Verdi's genius. Rossini's judgment has been triumphantly re-echoed ever since.

A Survey of Performances

When Verdi first considered composing *Rigoletto* for the Teatro San Carlo in Naples, the singers whom he had in mind for the roles of Gilda and Rigoletto were, as we have discovered from his letter to Vincenzo Flauto (*see* p. 10), Frezzolini and De Bassini. Erminia Frezzolini was certainly one of the composer's favourite sopranos in the decade preceding the composition of *Rigoletto*: she created the roles of Giselda in *I Lombardi* in 1843, and Giovanna in *Giovanna d'Arco* in 1845, both at La Scala, Milan. Presumably, a year later when Verdi had agreed to write the opera not for Naples but for Venice, Frezzolini was not available. At any rate, her name does not appear in the discussions concerning the casting of the Venice première. She did finally sing Gilda in the first Paris production of the opera in 1857 but, although she was then only thirty-nine, her voice was in decline: a French critic wrote of 'the grace of [this] élite soul which survived the weakening of her vocal organs'. She had also been the first New York Gilda in 1855, and was to retire from the stage in 1860.

The baritone Achille De Bassini was another singer whom Verdi greatly admired. Though he, too, was absent from the *Rigoletto* première, he had already created the leading baritone roles in three Verdi operas, *I due Foscari* (1844), *Il corsaro* (1848) and *Luisa Miller* (1849), and as late as 1862 was to travel to St Petersburg to sing Melitone in the first perfomance of *La forza del destino*.

In Venice, the three leading roles in *Rigoletto* were created by Felice Varesi (Rigoletto), Teresa Brambilla (Gilda) and Raffaele Mirate (Duke of Mantua). All three were among the leading singers of the day, and Varesi had been Verdi's first Macbeth in Florence four years earlier. Two years later he was also to be the first Germont *père* in *La traviata*. In 1851 he was thirty-eight years of age, and in his vocal prime. The tenor Raffaele Mirate, though in his mid-thirties, was a comparative newcomer but was already being spoken of approvingly, and Piave recommended him highly to Verdi. His performance as the Duke was satisfactory enough for Verdi to attempt, unsuccessfully, to engage him for his next opera, *Il trovatore*.

The only role which proved difficult to cast in Venice was that of Gilda. With Erminia Frezzolini unavailable, Verdi's choice fell upon Teresa De Giuli-Borsi who had sung in the

METROPOLITAN

OPERA HOUSE.

MR. HENRY E. ABBEY, - - - - · · · Director.
Acting Manager, - · · · · - MR. MAURICE GRAU.

Friday Evening, November 16. Twelfth Subscription Night,
VERDI'S OPERA

" RIGOLETTO."

IL DUCA..Sig. STAGNO
RIGOLETTO.............................Sig. GUADAGNINI
(His first appearance in America.)
SPARAFUCILE..................................Sig. NOVARA
MONTERONE.......................................M. AUGIER
MARULLO.......................................Sig. CONTINI
BORSA...Sig. GRAZZI
CEPRANO..Sig. CORSINI
MADALENA...................................Mme. SCALCHI
LA CONTESSA.................................Mme. GENETTI
GIOVANNA......................................Mlle FORTI
PAGGIO..Mlle. GOLDINI
AND
GILDA ....Mme. MARCELLA SEMBRICH

Musical Director and Conductor, - Sig. VIANESI

Weber Piano and Mason & Hamlin Organ Used.

All the above Operas performed at this House can be had in every form, Vocal and Instrumental at G. SCHIRMER, No. 35 Union Square, Importer and Publisher of Music.

The Scenery by Messrs. Fox, Schaeffer, Maeder, and Thompson.
The Costumes are entirely new, and were manufactured at Venice by D. Ascoli, under the supervision of Mr. Henry Dazian.
The Appointments by Mr. Bradwell.
Master Machinist, Mr. W. H. Gifford.
Perruquier, Mr. Ch. Meyer.
Stage Managers, Corani and Abbiati.

LEFT: *Programme of the first performance of the opera at the Metropolitan Opera House, New York, in 1883. (The first New York performance was in 1855 at the Academy of Music)*

83

première of *La battaglia di Legnano* in Rome in 1849. For some unclear reason the Fenice management did not wish to engage Giuli-Borsi, who sang Gilda elsewhere a year after the première (*see below*), and Verdi was determined not to have the theatre's candidate, Giulia Sanchioli. 'I have no wish to minimize the merits of Sanchioli,' Verdi wrote to Brenna, 'I fully grant her all that the world says of her. I merely say she will not succeed in my new opera.' Two or three other names were then proposed, among them that of Sofia Cruvelli. Verdi was to have trouble with this lady in Paris some years later, during the rehearsal period of *Les vêpres siciliennes* when she disappeared without warning for several days, and was found later to have gone off for an impromptu holiday with her lover. At this time, Verdi had still not heard Cruvelli. He had been given good reports of her singing, but also knew that she was an eccentric and capricious woman. 'I will tell you frankly', he wrote to Brenna, 'that I do not like these caricatures of Malibran, who have her eccentricities without her genius. Writing an opera for these weird brains is something that makes me tremble. Those parts they do not understand they simply neglect to study, and thus cause the opera to fail.'

The choice narrowed itself to two sopranos: the thirty-eight-year-old Teresa Brambilla, one of seven sisters all of whom were singers, and the twenty-three-year-old Virginia Boccabadati. Verdi had his doubts about both, but thought that Brambilla was probably the better singer of the two. In the event, Teresa Brambilla proved to be an almost perfect Gilda. The *Gazzetta di Venezia* said that 'she adorned her part with her customary grace, and with all the charm and expression of her voice. Her acting was intelligent and effective, and the amorous being whom she created will only with difficulty be reproduced by any other interpreter.'

Teresa de Giuli-Borsi first sang Gilda in Turin in February, 1852, and in Livorno during the summer. In September, when she was preparing to sing the role again, her husband Carlo Antonio Borsi had the temerity to write to Verdi, requesting that he compose an additional aria for her to introduce into *Rigoletto*. Verdi's reply is fascinating:

> If you could be persuaded that my talent was so limited that I did not know how to do better than I have done in *Rigoletto*,

RIGOLETTO;

A Lyric Drama, in Three Acts,

THE MUSIC BY

VERDI.

THE LIBRETTO EDITED AND TRANSLATED BY

MANFREDO MAGGIONI,

AS REPRESENTED AT THE

ROYAL ITALIAN OPERA.

PRINTED, PUBLISHED, AND SOLD EXCLUSIVELY

BY T. BRETTELL, RUPERT STREET, HAYMARKET,

TO BE HAD AT

The Royal Italian Opera;

ALSO OF

ALL THE PRINCIPAL BOOKSELLERS & MUSICSELLERS.

ONE SHILLING AND SIXPENCE.

LEFT: *Title-page of the libretto in English translation, sold at Covent Garden in 1853*

you would not have requested of me an aria for this opera. Miserable talent, you may say, and I agree, but there it is. Then, if this *Rigoletto* can stand as it is, a new aria would be superfluous. And where would one put it? Verses and notes can be provided, but unless they are at the right time and in the right place, they will never make any effect. We may know of a place, but God forbid! We should be flayed alive. We should need to show Gilda with the Duke in his bedroom! Do you understand me? Whatever one did, it would have to be a duet. A magnificent duet!! But the priests, the monks and the hypocrites would all cry scandal. Oh, how happy were the times when Diogenes could say in the public

RIGHT: *Giovanni Mario (1810–83), who sang the role of the Duke of Mantua in the first London production of the opera in 1853*

square to those who asked him what he was doing: '*Hominem quaero*!!' and so on.

As for the cavatina in the first act ['*Caro nome*'], I do not understand where you find any agility in it. Perhaps you have not understood the tempo, which should be an *allegretto molto lento*. At a moderate tempo, and sung quietly throughout, it should not be difficult. But to return to your first proposition, let me add that I conceived *Rigoletto* without arias, without finales, as a long string of duets, because this was how I wanted it. If anyone adds: 'But one could do this here, and that there' etc. etc., I reply: 'That would be fine, but I did not know how to do any better.'

LEFT: *Angiolino Bosio, who sang Gilda in the first Covent Garden production of* Rigoletto *in 1853*

OPPOSITE: *Enrico Caruso (1873–1921) as the Duke of Mantua*

When *Rigoletto* was first produced in London, at Covent Garden on May 14, 1853, the conductor was Michael Costa and the principals were Angiolina Bosio (Gilda), Giovanni Mario (Duke of Mantua) and Giorgio Ronconi (Rigoletto), all of whom were admired by the critics, though the opera was not. It was, however, an instant success with that real and final arbiter, the public, and has seldom since been long away from the Covent Garden stage. Among the famous Gildas who appeared in *Rigoletto* at Covent Garden were Adelina Patti, Emma Albani, Marcella Sembrich, Nellie Melba, Selma Kurz, Luisa Tetrazzini, Maria Ivogün (the teacher of Elisabeth Schwarzkopf), Lina Pagliughi, Erna Berger, Elisabeth Schwarzkopf, Hilde Gueden; and, in more recent years, Mattiwilda Dobbs, Joan Sutherland, Renata Scotto, Anna Moffo and Ileana Cotrubas. Interpreters of the title-role have included Victor Maurel, Maurice Renaud (who sang with Melba and Caruso), Antonio Scotti, Mario Sammarco, Mattia Battistini, Mariano Stabile, Paolo Silveri, Marko Rothmüller, Tito Gobbi and Ingvar Wixell. Tenors who have sung the Duke of Mantua at Covent Garden include Enrico Tamberlik, Fernando de Lucia, Alessandro Bonci, Enrico Caruso, John McCormack, Dino Borgioli, Joseph Hislop, Giacomo Lauri-Volpi, Beniamino Gigli, Nicolai Gedda and Alfredo Kraus.

Many of these singers also appeared in American productions of the opera. After the first New York production in 1855 at the Academy of Music, *Rigoletto* became as popular in New York as it was everywhere else. When Caruso made his Met début in 1903, it was as the Duke of Mantua, in a cast which included Marcella Sembrich and Antonio Scotti. Other notable interpreters at the Met have included Frances Alda, Amelita Galli-Curci, Lily Pons and Roberta Peters as Gilda; Mario Chamlee, Armand Tokatyan, Jan Peerce, Richard Tucker, Giuseppe di Stefano and Jussi Björling as the Duke; and Tita Ruffo, Giuseppe de Luca, Lawrence Tibbett, Leonard Warren, Robert Merrill, Ettore Bastianini and Sherill Milnes as Rigoletto.

Other famous interpreters include Toti dal Monte, Bidu Sayao, Maria Callas (Gilda); Alfred Piccaver, Tito Schipa, Carlo Bergonzi (Duke of Mantua); and Joseph Schwarz, Mario Basiola, Piero Capuccilli (Rigoletto).

The first complete recording of *Rigoletto* was issued by Columbia in 1916, on seventeen twelve-inch 78 rpm records. The principal singers were Cesare Formichi (Rigoletto), Giuseppe Taccani (Duke) and Ines Maria Ferraris (Gilda), and the orchestra and chorus of La Scala, Milan, were conducted by Guglielmo Somma. Neither this nor a recording made the following year by His Master's Voice (again, seventeen discs) is of much importance, for few of the singers were among the

OPPOSITE: *Lily Pons (1904–76) as Gilda, a role she sang at the Metropolitan Opera, New York, in the thirties and forties* LEFT: *Adelina Patti (1843–1919), a famous Gilda. An 1867 photograph*

91

leading exponents of these roles. The HMV cast is headed by
Giuseppe Danise (Rigoletto), Carlo Broccardi (Duke) and
Ayres Borghi-Zerni (Gilda), and the Scala forces are conducted
by Carlo Sabajno. Formichi (Columbia) was, in fact, an admired
Rigoletto, and the HMV Rigoletto, Danise, was a favourite at
the Met in the 1920s; but neither their contributions, nor those
of the other principals, are sufficiently commanding to make
one overlook the inadequacy of the recorded sound. The name
of Carlo Sabajno, HMV's conductor, is well known to
collectors of vocal records, for he accompanied a great many
singers' records in the twenties and thirties, and indeed was in
charge of recordings for the Italian branch of HMV (*La Voce del
Padrone*) for twenty-five years.

A third recording, made by *La Voce del Padrone* in 1928 on fifteen discs, is still of some interest today, and has been re-issued on LP. The Scala chorus and orchestra are again conducted by Sabajno, and the cast includes Luigi Piazza (Rigoletto), Lina Pagliughi (Gilda) and Tino Folgar (Duke). This was the first electrical (as oposed to acoustic) recording of *Rigoletto*, and the gain in clarity of sound is enormous. Sabajno conducts an authoritative performance, the young Spanish tenor Tino Folgar is an elegant, light-weight Duke, but the Rigoletto is somewhat crude. The great asset of this recording is the Gilda of the then twenty-year-old soprano Lina Pagliughi, who had made her operatic debut as Gilda only two months earlier, and had been immediately engaged by Sabajno for the

ABOVE: Rigoletto, *Act II at the Bavarian State Opera, Munich. Erica Köth (Gilda) and Thomas Tipton (Rigoletto)*

recording. The spontaneity of her interpretation is matched by the sweet timbre and freshness of her voice and by her already impeccable technique.

Columbia retaliated in 1930 with a fifteen-disc recording, in which Lorenzo Molajoli conducts the Scala chorus and orchestra, and the cast is headed by three well-known names of the period: Riccardo Stracciari (Rigoletto), Mercedes Capsir (Gilda) and Dino Borgioli (Duke). Stracciari, generally regarded as one of the finest Italian baritones of the century, was, however, fifty-nine at the time of the recording, and well past his best. The soprano is excellent, and Borgioli is a supple and musical Duke. This recording, too, has been re-issued on LP.

The next complete recording of *Rigoletto* in chronological sequence is a private, 'pirated' recording made from a Metropolitan Opera broadcast in 1939, when the principals were Lawrence Tibbett, Lily Pons and Jan Kiepura, and the conductor Gennaro Papi. The recording quality, not surprisingly, is poor, but the performance is fascinating for the light it throws on the style and customs of the time. Despite the occasional provincial mannerism, Tibbett's Rigoletto has great authority, and the sheer beauty of his voice is clearly revealed. Jan Kiepura was a popular matinée idol in Europe: rhythmically erratic, he nevertheless presents a Duke of charm and vocal finesse. Lily Pons is a typical coloratura Gilda, ending 'Caro nome' with an E in altissimo, but first-rate of her kind, with great virtuosity and a more colourful timbre than is usual with this type of voice.

A war-time (1944) Berlin performance has been re-issued on LP by *Deutsche Grammophon*. Sung in German, with Robert Heger conducting the chorus and orchestra of the Berlin Staatsoper, it boasts a superb cast, headed by Germany's leading Verdi baritone of the period, Heinrich Schlusnus. Though he was fifty-six in 1944, Schlusnus requires no allowances to be made for him: he is still a great singing-actor. The delightful Erna Berger, who sang Gilda in London and New York after the war, has the fresh, virginal quality which Gilda must display, at least in Act I! The prodigious Helge Roswaenge is a trifle heavy as the Duke, and his habitual scoop is in evidence, yet his too is a performance of great presence. Two other fine artists make their mark as Maddalena and Sparafucile:

LEFT: *Marcella Sembrich (1858–1935), who sang Gilda in the first Metropolitan performance of* Rigoletto *in 1883*

Margarete Klose and Josef Greindl.

All those recordings might properly be described as 'historical'. Since the advent of LP, there have been at least a further fifteen recordings of *Rigoletto* in Italian by major recording companies alone, to say nothing of recordings in various other languages, discs of excerpts and so on. None is perfect, but many are excellent and contain magnificent individual performances. They appear and disappear from catalogues, and are often re-issued on different and cheaper labels. The following are all worth consideration for one or more reasons, and each can easily be identified in record shops by the name of the conductor.

Leonard Warren, Erna Berger, Jan Peerce, conducted by Renato Cellini: based on Metropolitan Opera performances of around 1950, this is notable for the Rigoletto of Leonard Warren, the Met's successor to Lawrence Tibbett, and for the Gilda of Erna Berger, sounding just as young as in her Berlin recording, but this time in the right language. Jan Peerce lacks charm and vocal flexibility, but has his moments.

OPPOSITE: *Dame Nellie Melba (1861–1931) as Gilda, the role in which she made her operatic debut at the Théâtre de la Monaie, Brussels, in 1887*

Tito Gobbi, Maria Callas, Giuseppe di Stefano, conducted by Tullio Serafin: Gobbi was the most admired Rigoletto of his time, and his superb vocal acting and wide range of colour are excellently caught here, under Serafin's sympathetic and authoritative direction. Callas is mis-cast as Gilda, and Di Stefano is not exactly a Verdi stylist, but this set is essential hearing because of Gobbi.

Cornell MacNeil, Joan Sutherland, Renato Cioni, conducted by Nino Sanzogno: MacNeil is an acceptable Rigoletto in the Leonard Warren tradition, and Joan Sutherland a most affecting Gilda, her agile dramatic soprano probably closer in type of voice to what Verdi would have expected to hear than the equally agile lyric voices one often encounters in the role.

Giuseppe Taddei, Lina Pagliughi, Ferrucio Tagliavini, conducted by Angelo Questo: this comes closest to complete success. Taddei is an effective and intelligent Rigoletto, and the honeyed vocal charm of Tagliavini catches one aspect of the Duke. Pagliughi, a good quarter of a century on from her earlier recording, sounds almost as fresh. Hers is a most beautiful Gilda.

Robert Merrill, Roberta Peters, Jussi Björling, conducted by Jonel Perlea: a souvenir of Met performances of the fifties, this fails to come alive as a performance, though there is much to admire in Merrill's Rigoletto and Björling's Duke, musically if not dramatically.

Aldo Protti, Hilde Gueden, Mario del Monaco, conducted by Alberto Erede: Gueden was a most moving Gilda in the opera house, and she sings superlatively on this recording. Unfortunately, Protti is a dull Rigoletto and Del Monaco a blustery Duke, and Erede fails to impose himself upon the performance.

Dietrich Fischer-Dieskau, Renata Scotto, Carlo Bergonzi, conducted by Rafael Kubelik: though Fischer-Dieskau sings with the intelligence and style one expects from him, his vocal quality makes him an unconvincing Rigoletto. Bergonzi is an

97

elegant and persuasive Duke, and Scotto could hardly be bettered as Gilda.

Cornell MacNeil, Reri Grist, Nicolai Gedda, conducted by Francesco Molinari-Pradelli: MacNeil is less good than in his earlier recording, and the delightful Reri Grist occasionally sounds thin and colourless. Gedda's Duke is exemplary, both elegant and fiery, and faultless in enunciation of the text.

Sherill Milnes, Joan Sutherland, Luciano Pavarotti, conducted by Richard Bonynge: Sutherland's second Gilda is even more convincing than her first, but Milnes is disappointing and Pavarotti offers more enthusiasm than finesse.

Libretto

TIME: THE SIXTEENTH CENTURY
PLACE: MANTUA

English translation by Charles Osborne

SCENA PRIMA

SCENE I

Sala magnifica nel palazzo Ducale con porte nel fondo che mettono ad altre sale, pure splendidamente illuminate.
Folla di Cavalieri e Dame in gran costume nel fondo delle sale; Paggi che vanno e vengono. La feste è nel suo pieno. Musica interna da lontano.

A splendid hall in the ducal palace, with doors at the back into other rooms all brilliantly lit. Sumptuously costumed courtiers and ladies in the background; pages pass to and fro. The festivities are at their height. Music can be heard in the distance.

DUCA

DUKE

Della mia bella incognita borghese
Toccare il fin dell'avventura io voglio.

I shall soon bring to a head my adventure
With that unknown beauty in the town.

BORSA

BORSA

Di quella giovan che vedete al tempio?

The young one whom you see in church?

DUCA

DUKE

Da tre mesi ogni festa.

Every Sunday for the last three months.

BORSA

BORSA

La sua dimora?

Where does she live?

DUCA

DUKE

In un remoto calle;
Misterïoso un uom v'entra ogni notte.

In a remote lane;
A man enters there secretly every night.

BORSA

BORSA

E sa colei chi sia
L'amante suo?

And does she know who her admirer
is?

DUCA

DUKE

Lo ignora.

She does not.

(Un gruppo di Dame e Cavalieri attraversano la sala)

(A group of ladies and courtiers crosses the hall)

BORSA

BORSA

Quante beltà! Mirate.

So much beauty! Look.

DUCA

Le vince tutte di Cepran la sposa.

BORSA

(piano)

Non v'oda il Conte, o Duca!

DUCA

A me che importa?

BORSA

Dirlo ad altra ei potria.

DUCA

Né sventura per me certo saria.
Questa o quella per me pari sono
A quant'altre d'intorno mi vedo;
Del mio core l'impero non cedo
Meglio ad una che ad altra beltà.
La costoro avvenenza è qual dono
Di che il fato ne infiora la vita;
S'oggi questa mi torna gradita
Forse un'altra doman lo sarà.
La costanza, tiranna del core,
Detestiamo qual morbo crudele.
Sol chi vuole si serbi fedele;
Non v'ha amor se non v'è libertà.
De' mariti geloso il furore,
Degli amanti le smanie derido;
Anco d'Argo i cent'occhi disfido
Se mi punge una qualche beltà.

(alla signora di Ceprano movendo ad incontrarla con molta galanteria:)

Partite? Crudele!

CONTESSA DI CEPRANO

Seguire lo sposo
M'è forza a Ceprano.

DUKE

Ceprano's wife outshines them all.

BORSA

(softly)

Don't let the Count hear you, my Lord.

DUKE

What do I care?

BORSA

He might tell some other lady.

DUKE

What a misfortune for me that would
be.
This or that one, they all seem the same
to me.
As the others I see around me;
I don't give my heart
More to one beauty than to another.
Their charm is the gift
With which fate enhances life.
If one finds favour with me today,
perhaps tomorrow it will be another.
Constancy, that tyranny of the heart
I detest as though it were the plague.
Let him who wishes to, be faithful;
You can't have love without freedom.
The jealous rage of husbands,
And the frenzies of lovers, I mock at;
I would even challenge the hundred
eyes of Argus
When I am roused by some beauty.

(To the Countess Ceprano, moving to her side with a great show of gallantry:)

You're leaving? Cruel one!

COUNTESS CEPRANO:

I have to return to Ceprano
With my husband.

DUCA

Ma dee luminoso
In corte tal astro qual sole brillare.
Per voi qui ciascuno dovrà palpitare.
Per voi già possente la fiamma d'amore
Inebria, conquide, distrugge il mio core.

(con enfasi baciandole la mano)

CONTESSA DI CEPRANO

Calmatevi!

DUCA

No.

(Le dà il braccio ed esce con lei)

RIGOLETTO

(che s'incontra nel signor di Ceprano:)

In testa che avete,
Signor di Ceprano?

(Il Conte di Ceprano fa un gesto
d'impazienza e segue il Duca)

RIGOLETTO

(ai Cortigiani)

Ei sbuffa, vedete?

BORSA E CORO

Che festa!

RIGOLETTO

Oh sì!

BORSA E CORO

Il Duca qui pur si diverte!

RIGOLETTO

Così non è sempre? Che nuove
scoperte!

DUKE

But such luminous beauty
Should shine here at court like the sun.
You have conquered the hearts of all here.
Already kindled by you, the flame of love
Intoxicates, conquers and overwhelms my heart.

(He kisses her hand passionately)

COUNTESS CEPRANO

Calm yourself.

DUKE

No.

(He gives her his arm, and escorts her out)

RIGOLETTO

(Enters and addresses Count Ceprano:)

What are you thinking about,
My lord Ceprano?

(Count Ceprano gives an impatient gesture,
and follows the Duke)

RIGOLETTO

(To the Courtiers)

He's furious, you see?

BORSA AND CHORUS

What fun!

RIGOLETTO

Oh, yes.

BORSA AND CHORUS

The Duke is amusing himself here.

RIGOLETTO

Doesn't he always? What new
escapades!

Il giuoco ed il vino, le feste, la danza,
Battaglie, conviti, ben tutto gli sta.
Or della Contessa l'assedio egli avanza.
E intanto il marito fremendo ne va.

(esce)

MARULLO

(Premuroso)

Gran nuova! Gran nuova!

CORO

Che avvenne? Parlate!

MARULLO

Stupir ne dovrete.

CORO

Narrate, narrate!

MARULLO

(redendo)

Ah! ah! Rigoletto . . .

CORO

Ebben?

MARULLO

Caso enorme!

CORO

Perduto ha la gobba?
Non è più difforme?

MARULLO

Più strana è la cosa! Il pazzo possiede . . .

CORO

Infine?

Gambling, drinking, parties, dancing,
Battles and feasts, he enjoys them all.
Now he's going to lay siege to the Countess
While her husband stands by, fuming.

(Exit)

MARULLO

(Entering eagerly)

Great news, great news!

CHORUS

What's happened? Speak.

MARULLO

You'll be astonished.

CHORUS

Tell us, tell us.

MARULLO

(Laughing)

Ha, ha, Rigoletto . . .

CHORUS

Well?

MARULLO

It's something extraordinary.

CHORUS

Has he lost his hunch?
He's no longer deformed?

MARULLO

It's stranger than that. The idiot has . . .

CHORUS

What, then?

MARULLO	MARULLO
Un'amante.	A mistress
CORO	CHORUS
Un'amante! Chi il crede?	A mistress? Who'd believe it!
MARULLO	MARULLO
Il gobbo in Cupido or s'è trasformato.	The hunchback has turned into Cupid.
CORO	CHORUS
Quel mostro Cupido? Cupido beato!	That monster, Cupid? A charming Cupid!
DUCA	DUKE
(a Rigoletto)	*(To Rigoletto, as they re-enter together)*
Ah, più di Ceprano importuno non v'è! La cara sua sposa è un angiol per me!	There's no one more tedious than Ceprano. His dear wife is an angel to me!
RIGOLETTO	RIGOLETTO
Rapitela.	Abduct her.
DUCA	DUKE
È detto; ma il farlo?	Easily said, but how to do it?
RIGOLETTO	RIGOLETTO
Stasera.	This evening.
DUCA	DUKE
Non pensi tu al Conte?	You've forgotten about the Count.
RIGOLETTO	RIGOLETTO
Non c'è la prigione?	What about prison?
DUCA	DUKE
Ah, no.	Ah, no.
RIGOLETTO	RIGOLETTO
Ebben, s'esilia.	Well, then, exile.
DUCA	DUKE
Nemmeno, buffone.	Nor that either, fool.

RIGOLETTO

Allora la testa . . .

(indicando di farla tagliare)

CONTE DI CEPRANO

(tra se)

Oh l'anima nera!

DUCA

(battendo con la mano una spalla al Conte)

Che di', questa testa?

RIGOLETTO

È ben naturale.
Che far di tal testa?
A che cosa ella vale?

CONTE DI CEPRANO

(infuriato, brandendo la spada)

Marrano!

DUCA

(a Ceprano)

Fermate!

RIGOLETTO

Da rider mi fa.

CORO

(tra loro)

In furia è montato!

DUCA

(a Rigoletto)

Buffone, vien qua.
Ah, sempre tu spingi lo scherzo
all'estremo.
Quell'ira che sfidi colpir ti potrà.

RIGOLETTO

What about his head?

(Makes a gesture of cutting it off)

COUNT CEPRANO

(To himself)

Oh, black-hearted villain!

DUKE

(Tapping the Count on the shoulder)

What do you say? This head?

RIGOLETTO

It's quite natural.
What can you do with a head like that?
What's it good for?

COUNT CEPRANO

(Furious, drawing his sword)

Scoundrel!

DUKE

(To Ceprano)

That's enough!

RIGOLETTO

He makes me laugh.

CHORUS

(To themselves)

He's furious now.

DUKE

(To Rigoletto)

Come here, fool.
You always carry a joke to extremes.
The anger you arouse may be your
undoing.

RIGOLETTO

Che coglier mi puote? Di loro non
temo.
Del Duca il protetto nessun toccherà.

CONTE DI CEPRANO

(ai Cortigiani a parte)

Vendetta del pazzo!

CORO

Contr'esso un rancore
Pei tristi suoi modi di noi chi non ha?

CONTE DI CEPRANO

Vendetta!

CORO

Ma come?

CONTE DI CEPRANO

Stanotte, chi ha core
Sia in armi da me.

TUTTI

Sì.

BORSA E CORO

A notte.

TUTTI

Sarà.

(La folla dei danzatori invade la scena)

Tutto è gioia, tutto è festa,
Tutto invitaci a goder!
Oh, guardate, non par questa
Or la reggia del piacer?

CONTE DI MONTERONE

(dall'interno)

Ch'io gli parli.

RIGOLETTO

What harm can come to me? I'm not
afraid of them.
No one would touch the Duke's favourite.

COUNT CEPRANO

(Aside, to the Courtiers)

Revenge on the madman.

CHORUS

Which of us hasn't a grudge against him
For his malicious ways?

COUNT CEPRANO

Vengeance!

CHORUS

But how?

COUNT CEPRANO

Tonight, those of you who are daring,
Meet me, armed.

ALL

Yes.

BORSA AND CHORUS

Tonight.

ALL

So be it!

(A crowd of dancers enters)

All is joy and festivity,
Everything invites us to pleasure!
Oh see, is this not
A palace of revelry?

COUNT MONTERONE

(Outside)

Let me speak to him.

DUCA

No.

CONTE DI MONTERONE

(entrando)

Il voglio.

TUTTI

Monterone!

CONTE DI MONTERONE

(fissando el Duca, con nobile orgoglio)

Sì, Monteron . . . la voce mia qual tuono
Vi scuoterà dovunque.

RIGOLETTO

(al Duca, contraffacendo la voce di Monterone)

Ch'io gli parli.

(Si avanza con ridicola gravità)

Voi congiuraste contro noi, signore,
E noi, clementi invero, perdonammo.
Qual vi piglia or delirio a tutte l'ore
Di vostra figlia a reclamar l'onore?

CONTE DI MONTERONE

(guardando Rigoletto con ira sprezzante)

Novello insulto! Ah sì, a turbare . . .

(al Duca)

Sarò vostr'orgie . . . verrò a gridare
Fino a che vegga restarsi inulto
Di mia famiglia l'atroce insulto;
E se al carnefice pur mi darete,
Spettro terribile mi rivedrete,
Portante in mano il teschio mio,
Vendetta chiedere al mondo e a Dio.

DUKE

No.

COUNT MONTERONE

(Entering)

I insist.

ALL

Monterone!

COUNT MONTERONE

(His gaze fixed with noble pride upon the Duke)

Yes, Monterone . . . my voice, like thunder,
Will shake you, wherever you are.

RIGOLETTO

(To the Duke, imitating Monterone's voice)

Let me speak to him.

(He advances upon Monterone with mock solemnity)

You conspired against us, sir,
And we, in true clemency, forgave you.
What madness seizes you to complain
Continually about your daughter's honour?

COUNT MONTERONE

(Giving Rigoletto a look of contemptuous anger)

A further insult. Ah yes, I'll interrupt

(To the Duke)

Your orgies . . . I'll raise my voice
As long as the monstrous insult
To my family remains unavenged
And, even if you give me to the executioner,
My dreadful spectre will return,
Carrying my head in its hand,
Calling to the world, to God, for vengeance.

DUCA

Non più, arrestatelo.

RIGOLETTO

È matto.

CORO

Quai detti!

CONTE DI MONTERONE

(al Duca e Rigoletto)

Oh, siate entrambi voi maledetti.
Slanciare il cane a leon morente
È vile, o Duca,

(a Rigoletto)

E tu, serpente,
Tu che d'un padre ridi al dolore,
Sii maledetto!

RIGOLETTO

(tra sè, colpito)

Che sento! Orrore!

TUTTI

(meno Rigoletto)

O tu che la festa, audace, hai turbato,
Da un genio d'inferno qui fosti guidato;
È vano ogni detto, di qua t'allontana,
Va, trema, o vegliardo, dell'ira sovrana.
Tu l'hai provocata, più speme non v'è.
Un'ora fatale fu questa per te.

*(Il Conte di Monterone parte fra due alabar-
dieri; tutti gli altri seguono il Duca in altra
stanza)*

DUKE

Enough! Arrest him.

RIGOLETTO

He's mad.

CHORUS

What words!

COUNT MONTERONE

(To the Duke and Rigoletto)

Ah, may you both be cursed.
To set your dog upon a dying lion
Is vile, oh Duke,

(To Rigoletto)

And you, serpent,
You who laugh at a father's grief,
My curse upon you.

RIGOLETTO

(To himself, overcome)

What do I hear? Oh, horror!

ALL

(Except Rigoletto)

Oh you who have dared to disturb our
festivities,
Guided here by a spirit from hell,
All your words are vain, depart from here.
Go, old man, fear your sovereign's wrath.
You have provoked it, and there is no
hope for you.
This has been a fatal hour for you.

*(Exit Monterone between two halberdiers.
The others follow the Duke into another
room)*

SCENA SECONDA

*L'estremità d'una via cieca. A sinistra, una
casa di discreta apparenza con una piccola
corte circondata da mura. Nella corte un
grosso ed alto albero ed un sedile di marmo;
nel muro, una porta che mette alla strada;
sopra il muro, un terrazzo praticabile,
sostenuto da arcate. La porta del primo
piano dà sul detto terrazzo, a cui si ascende
per una scala di fronte. A destra della via è
il muro altissimo del giardino e un fianco del
palazzo di Ceprano. È notte.*

*Entra Rigoletto chiuso nel suo mantello;
Sparafucile lo segue, portando sotto il
mantello una lunga spada.*

RIGOLETTO

(tra sé)

Quel vecchio maledivami!

SPARAFUCILE

Signor?

RIGOLETTO

Va', non ho niente.

SPARAFUCILE

Nè chiesi. A voi presente
Un uom di spada sta.

RIGOLETTO

Un ladro?

SPARAFUCILE

Un uom che libera
Per poco da un rivale.
E voi ne avete.

RIGOLETTO

Quale?

SCENE II

*The end of a cul-de-sac. On the left, a house
of modest appearance with a small courtyard
surrounded by a wall. In the courtyard a huge
tree and a marble bench. A door in the wall
leads to the street. Above the wall, a
practical terrace supported by arches. The
first-floor door gives onto this terrace, reached
by a stair-case in front. On the right of the
street is a high garden wall, and the side of
Ceprano's palace. It is night.*

*Rigoletto enters, his cloak wrapped around
him. Sparafucile follows him, carrying a long
sword beneath his cloak.*

RIGOLETTO

(To himself)

That old man cursed me!

SPARAFUCILE

Sir?

RIGOLETTO

Go away, I have nothing for you.

SPARAFUCILE

I haven't asked for anything. You see
before you
A swordsman.

RIGOLETTO

A thief?

SPARAFUCILE

A man who would rid you
Of a rival, for a fee.
You surely have a rival.

RIGOLETTO

Who?

SPARAFUCILE

La vostra donna è là.

RIGOLETTO

(tra sé)

Che sento!

(forte)

E quanto spendere
Per un signor dovrei?

SPARAFUCILE

Prezzo maggior vorrei.

RIGOLETTO

Com'usasi pagar?

SPARAFUCILE

Una metà s'anticipa,
Il resto si dà poi.

RIGOLETTO

(tra sé)

Demonio!

(forte)

E come puoi
Tanto securo oprar?

SPARAFUCILE

Soglio in cittade uccidere,
Oppure nel mio tetto.
L'uomo di sera aspetto;
Una stoccata e muor.

RIGOLETTO

(tra sé)

Demonio!

(forte)

E come in casa?

SPARAFUCILE

Your mistress lives here.

RIGOLETTO

(To himself)

What do I hear?

(aloud)

And how much would it cost
For a nobleman?

SPARAFUCILE

That would cost more.

RIGOLETTO

How are you paid, usually?

SPARAFUCILE

Half in advance,
The rest afterwards.

RIGOLETTO

(To himself)

Demon!

(Aloud)

And how is it
You can operate so safely?

SPARAFUCILE

I kill either in the town
Or under my own roof.
I wait for the man at night;
One thrust and he's dead.

RIGOLETTO

(To himself)

Demon!

(Aloud)

How, exactly, in your own house?

SPARAFUCILE

È facile,
M'aiuta mia sorella;
Per le vie danza, è bella,
Chi voglio attira, e allor . . .

RIGOLETTO

Comprendo.

SPARAFUCILE

Senza strepito.

RIGOLETTO

Comprendo.

SPARAFUCILE

È questo il mio strumento,

(*Mostra la spada*)

Vi serve?

RIGOLETTO

No, al momento.

SPARAFUCILE

Peggio per voi.

RIGOLETTO

Chi sa?

SPARAFUCILE

Sparafucil mi nomino.

RIGOLETTO

Straniero?

SPARAFUCILE

Borgognone.

RIGOLETTO

E dove all'occasione?

SPARAFUCILE

It's easy.
My sister helps me:
She dances in the streets, she's beautiful,
She entices them, and then . . .

RIGOLETTO

I understand.

SPARAFUCILE

Without a sound.

RIGOLETTO

I understand.

SPARAFUCILE

And this is my instrument.

(*Displays his sword*)

Can I serve you?

RIGOLETTO

Not at present.

SPARAFUCILE

So much the worse for you.

RIGOLETTO

But who knows?

SPARAFUCILE

Sparafucile's my name.

RIGOLETTO

A foreigner?

SPARAFUCILE

Burgundian.

RIGOLETTO

And where, if I have need of you?

SPARAFUCILE

Qui sempre a sera.

RIGOLETTO

Va.

SPARAFUCILE

Sparafucil . . . Sparafucil . . .

RIGOLETTO

Va . . . va . . . va . . . va.

(Sparafucile parte)

RIGOLETTO

(guardando dietro a Sparafucile)

Pari siamo!
Io la lingua, egli ha il pugnale;
L'uomo son io che ride,
Ei quel che spegne!
Quel vecchio maledivami!
O uomini! O natura!
Vil scellerato mi faceste voi!
O rabbia! Esser difforme!
O rabbia! Esser buffone!
Non dover, non poter altro che ridere!

Il retaggio, d'ogni uom m'è tolto: il
pianto!
Questo padrone mio,
Giovin, giocondo, sì possente, bello,
Sonnecchiando mi dice:
Fa' ch'io rida, buffone!
Forzarmi deggio e farlo!
Oh dannazione!
Odio a voi, cortigiani schernitori!
Quanta in mordervi ho gioia!
Se iniquo son, per cagion vostra è solo.
Ma in altr'uomo qui mi cangio!
Quel vecchio maledivami! Tal pensiero
Perché conturba ognor la mente mia?
Mi coglierà sventura?
Ah no, è follia!

SPARAFUCILE

I'm always here in the evenings.

RIGOLETTO

Go.

SPARAFUCILE

Sparafucile, Sparafucile.

RIGOLETTO

Go . . . go . . . go . . . go.

(Exit Sparafucile)

RIGOLETTO

(Looking after Sparafucile)

We are similar!
I have my tongue, he has his dagger;
I am a man who laughs,
And he one who slays!
That old man cursed me!
Oh men! Oh nature!
You have made me a vile scoundrel!
Oh torment! To be deformed!
Oh torment! To be a jester!
To be forced to, to be able to do
nothing but laugh!
Tears, the consolation of all men,
Are denied me!
That master of mine
Young, jovial, powerful, handsome,
Lazily says to me
'Make me laugh, jester!'
And I must force myself to do it.
Oh damnation!
I hate you, sneering courtiers!
How I enjoy stinging you!
If I am wicked, it's all because of you.
But here I become a different man!
That old man cursed me! That thought,
Why does it continue to disturb my mind?
Does some misfortune threaten me?
Ah, no, this is madness!

*(Apre con chiave ed entra nel cortile.
Gilda esce dalla casa e si getta nelle sue
braccia)*

RIGOLETTO

Figlia!

GILDA

Mio padre!

RIGOLETTO

A te d'appresso
Trova sol gioia il core oppresso.

GILDA

Oh, quanto amore!

RIGOLETTO

Mia vita sei!
Senza te in terra qual bene avrei?

(sospira)

GILDA

Voi sospirate! Che v'ange tanto?
Lo dite a questa povera figlia.
Se v'ha mistero, per lei sia franto,
Ch'ella conosca la sua famiglia.

RIGOLETTO

Tu non ne hai.

GILDA

Qual nome avete?

RIGOLETTO

A te che importa?

GILDA

Se non volete
Di voi parlarmi . . .

*(He opens the door with a key, and enters the
courtyard. Gilda comes out of the house, and
throws herself into his arms)*

RIGOLETTO

Daughter!

GILDA

My father!

RIGOLETTO

When I am near you,
My oppressed heart finds its only joy.

GILDA

Oh, such love!

RIGOLETTO

You are my life!
Without you, what good would life
hold for me?

(He sighs)

GILDA

You sigh. What is upsetting you?
Tell your poor daughter.
If you have a secret, share it with her,
Tell her something of her own family.

RIGOLETTO

You have none.

GILDA

What is your real name?

RIGOLETTO

What does that matter to you?

GILDA

If you do not wish
To speak of yourself . . .

RIGOLETTO

(interrompendola)

Non uscir mai.

GILDA

Non vo che al tempio.

RIGOLETTO

Oh ben tu fai.

GILDA

Se non di voi, almen chi sia
Fate ch'io sappia la madre mia.

RIGOLETTO

Ah, deh, non parlare al misero
Del suo perduto bene.
Ella sentia, quell'angelo,
Pietà delle mie pene.
Solo, difforme, povero,
Per compassion mi amò.
Ah, morìa. Le zolle coprano
Lievi quel capo amato.
Sola or tu resti al misero.
O Dio, sii ringraziato!

GILDA

(singhiozzando)

Oh, quanto dolor! Chi spremere
Sì amaro pianto può?
Padre, non più, calmatevi.
Mi lacera tal vista.
Il nome vostro ditemi,
Il duol che sì v'attrista.

RIGOLETTO

A che nomarmi? È inutile!
Padre ti sono, è basti.
Me forse al mondo temono,
D'alcuno ho forse gli asti,
Altri mi maledicono.

RIGOLETTO

(Interrupting her)

Don't ever go out.

GILDA

I go only to church.

RIGOLETTO

You have done well.

GILDA

If not about you, at least let me know
About my mother.

RIGOLETTO

Ah, don't speak to a wretched man
Of his past happiness.
That angel felt
Pity for my sorrows.
Alone, deformed, poor,
She loved me out of compassion.
Alas, she died. The unfeeling earth
Covers that beloved head.
Now you alone remain to this wretched man.
Oh God, be thanked!

GILDA

(Sobbing)

Oh, what sadness! What can cause
Such bitter tears?
Father, no more, calm yourself.
I cannot bear to see you like this.
Tell my your name
And why you are so sad.

RIGOLETTO

Tell you my name? That's useless.
I am your father, that's enough.
In this world I am mostly feared,
Perhaps resented by some
And cursed by others.

GILDA

Patria, parenti, amici,
Voi dunque non avete?

RIGOLETTO

Patria! parenti! amici!

(con effusione)

Culto, famiglia, la patria,
Il mio universo è in te!

GILDA

Ah, se può lieto rendervi,
Gioia è la vita a me!
Già da tre lune son qui venuta
Nè la cittade ho ancor veduta;
Se il concedete, farlo or potrei.

RIGOLETTO

Mai! mai! Uscita, dimmi, unqua sei?

GILDA

No.

RIGOLETTO

Guai!

GILDA

(tra sé)

Ah, che dissi!

RIGOLETTO

Ben te ne guarda!

(tra sé)

Potrien seguirla, rapirla ancora!
Qui d'un buffone si disonora
La figlia, e se ne ride. Orror!

(verso la casa:)

Olà?

GILDA

Country, relations, friends,
Have you none of these?

RIGOLETTO

Country, relations, friends!

(Effusively)

Religion, family, country,
My entire universe is you!

GILDA

Ah, if I can make you happy,
Life is a joy to me!
I have been here for three months,
And haven't yet seen the city.
If you permit it, I could do so now.

RIGOLETTO

Never, never! Tell me,
Have you ever gone out?

GILDA

No.

RIGOLETTO

Beware!

GILDA

(To herself)

Ah, what have I said?

RIGOLETTO

Take care that you don't!

(To himself)

They could follow her, even abduct her!
Here, they would dishonour a jester's
Daughter, and laugh about it. Horror!

(He calls towards the house:)

Hey, there!

(Giovanna esce dalla casa.)

GIOVANNA

Signor?

RIGOLETTO

Venendo mi vede alcuno?
Bada, di' il vero.

GIOVANNA

Ah no, nessuno.

RIGOLETTO

Sta ben. La porta che dà al bastione
È sempre chiusa?

GIOVANNA

Ognor si sta.

RIGOLETTO

(a Giovanna)

Veglia, o donna, questo fiore
Che a te puro confidai;
Veglia attenta, e non sia mai
Che s'offuschi il suo candor.
Tu dei venti dal furore,
Ch'altri fiori hanno piegato,
Lo difendi, e immacolato
Lo ridona al genitor.

GILDA

Quanto affetto, quali cure!
Che temete, padre mio?
Lassù in cielo presso Dio,
Veglia un angiol protettor.
Da noi toglie le sventure
Di mia madre il priego santo;
Non fia mai disvelto o franto
Questo a voi diletto fior.

(Il Duca in costume borghese dalla strada)

(Giovanna comes from the house)

GIOVANNA

Sir?

RIGOLETTO

Did anyone see me coming here?
Take care to tell me the truth.

GIOVANNA

Ah no, no one.

RIGOLETTO

Good. The door onto the terrace,
It's always shut?

GIOVANNA

Always.

RIGOLETTO

(To Giovanna)

Guard, oh woman, this chaste flower
Whom I have entrusted to you.
Watch over her carefully, and never
Let her innocence be sullied.
From the fury of the winds
Which has caused other flowers to droop,
Defend her, and give her back spotless
To her father.

GILDA

Such affection, such care.
What are you afraid of, father?
Up there in heaven, close to God,
A guardian angel watches over me.
We are protected from misfortune
By my mother's sacred prayers.
Never uprooted or crushed
Will this, your favourite flower, be.

_(The Duke, dressed as a commoner, appears
in the street outside)_

RIGOLETTO

Alcun v'è fuori.

*(Apre la porta della corte e, mentre esce a
guardar sulla strada, il Duca guizza furtivo
nella corte e si nasconde dietro l'albero;
gettando a Giovanna una borsa, la fa tacere)*

GILDA

Cielo! Sempre novel sospetto.

RIGOLETTO

(a Gilda, tornando)

Alla chiesa vi seguiva mai nessuno?

GILDA

Mai.

DUCA

(tra sé)

Rigoletto!

RIGOLETTO

Se talor qui picchian,
Guardatevi d'aprire.

GIOVANNA

Nemmeno al Duca?

RIGOLETTO

Non che ad altri a lui!
Mia figlia, addio.

DUCA

(tra sé)

Sua figlia!

GILDA

Addio, mio padre.

RIGOLETTO

There's someone outside.

*(He opens the door of the courtyard. As he
goes to look into the street, the Duke slips
furtively into the courtyard, hiding behind the
tree and throwing a purse to Giovanna, to
keep her quiet)*

GILDA

Heavens! Always some new suspicion.

RIGOLETTO

(Returning to Gilda)

Has anyone ever followed you to church?

GILDA

Never.

DUKE

(To himself)

Rigoletto!

RIGOLETTO

If anyone ever knocks,
Be careful not to open.

GIOVANNA

Not even to the Duke?

RIGOLETTO

Least of all to him!
My daughter, farewell.

DUKE

(To himself)

His daughter!

GILDA

Farewell, my father.

RIGOLETTO

Ah, veglia, o donna . . .

GILDA

Oh quanto affetto . . .

(S'abbracciano e Rigoletto parte chiudendosi
dietro la porta)

GILDA

Giovanna, ho dei rimorsi.

GIOVANNA

E perchè mai?

GILDA

Tacqui che un giovin ne seguiva al
tempio.

GIOVANNA

Perchè ciò dirgli?
L'odïate dunque cotesto giovin voi?

GILDA

No, no, chè troppo è bello e spira
amore.

GIOVANNA

E magnanimo sembra e gran signore.

GILDA

Signor nè principe io lo vorrei;
Sento che povero più l'amerei.
Sognando o vigile sempre lo chiamo,
E l'alma in estasi gli dice: t'a . . .

DUCA

(Esce improvviso, fa cenno a Giovanna
d'andarsene, e inginocchiandosi ai piedi di
Gilda termina la frase)

RIGOLETTO

Ah, guard, oh woman . . .

GILDA

Such affection . . .

(They embrace, and Rigoletto leaves, closing
the door behind him)

GILDA

Giovanna, I feel remorseful.

GIOVANNA

But why?

GILDA

I didn't tell him about the young man
Who follows me to the church.

GIOVANNA

Why should you tell him?
Do you dislike this young man, then?

GILDA

No, no, he's too handsome. He inspires
my love.

GIOVANNA

He seems generous, and a great gentleman.

GILDA

I don't want him to be a gentleman or a prince;
I think I'd love him more if he were poor.
Dreaming or awake, I'm always calling him,
And my spirit in ecstasy tells him: 'I lo—'

DUKE

(Emerges suddenly, signals to Giovanna to go
away, and kneeling at Gilda's feet concludes
her phrase)

T'amo!
T'amo; ripetilo sì caro accento;
Un puro schiudimi ciel di contento!

GILDA

Giovanna! Giovanna!
Ahi, misera! Non v'è più alcuno
Che qui rispondami! Oh Dio! nessuno?

DUCA

Son io coll'anima, che ti rispondo;
Ah, due che s'amano, son tutto un
mondo!

GILDA

Chi mai, chi giungere vi fece a me?

DUCA

Se angelo o demone, che importa a te?
Io t'amo.

GILDA

Uscitene.

DUCA

Uscire! Adesso!
Ora che accendene un fuoco istesso!
Ah, inseparabile d'amore il Dio
Stringeva, o vergine, tuo fato al mio!
È il sol dell'anima, la vita è amore,
Sua voce è il palpito del nostro core.
E fama e gloria, potenza e trono,
Umane, fragili qui cose sono.
Una pur avvene sola, divina:
È amor che agli angeli più ne avvicina!
Adunque amiamoci, donna celeste;
D'invidia agli uomini sarò per te.

GILDA

(tra sé)

Ah, de' miei vergini sogni son queste
Le voci tenere sì care a me!

I love you.
I love you: say it again in your sweet voice;
Reveal to me a heaven of delight.

GILDA

Giovanna! Giovanna!
Ah, unhappy girl, is there no one
To answer me? Oh God, no one?

DUKE

I am here, and my spirit replies to you:
Ah, two people in love are an entire
world.

GILDA

Who was it who brought you here to me?

DUKE

Whether it was an angel or a demon,
what does it matter? I love you.

GILDA

You must go.

DUKE

Go? Now?
Now that such a fire is burning within me?
Ah, the god of love has inseparably bound
Your fate to mine, oh maiden.
Love is the sunshine of my soul, it is life itself.
Its voice is the beating of our hearts.
Fame and glory, power and the throne,
These things are but earthly and frail.
One thing alone is divine:
Love, which brings us close to the angels!
Then let us love each other, divine woman;
You will make me the envy of all men.

GILDA

(To herself)

Ah, these are the tender sounds so dear to me
From my innocent dreams.

(Ceprano e Borsa compaiono sulla via)	*(Ceprano and Borsa appear in the street outside)*

DUCA

Che m'ami, deh, ripetimi.

GILDA

L'udiste.

DUCA

Oh, me felice!

GILDA

Il nome vostro ditemi.
Saperlo non mi lice?

CONTE DI CEPRANO

(a Borsa dalla via)

Il loco è qui.

DUCA

(pensando)

Mi nomino . . .

BORSA

(a Ceprano)

Sta ben . . .

(partono)

DUCA

Gualtier Maldè . . .
Studente sono . . . e povero.

GIOVANNA

(tornando spaventata)

Rumor di passi è fuori.

GILDA

Forse mio padre?

DUKE

Ah, say again that you love me.

GILDA

You have heard me.

DUKE

Oh, I'm so happy.

GILDA

Tell me your name.
May I not know it?

COUNT CEPRANO

(To Borsa, in the street)

This is the place.

DUKE

(Thinking)

My name is . . .

BORSA

(To Ceprano)

Good . . .

(They leave)

DUKE

. . . Walter Maldé
I'm a student . . . and poor.

GIOVANNA

(Returning, frightened)

There's a sound of footsteps outside.

GILDA

Perhaps it's my father?

DUCA

(tra sé)

Ah, cogliere
Potessi il traditore
Che sì mi sturba!

GILDA

(a Giovanna)

Acducilo di qua al bastione.
Or ite.

DUCA

Di', m'amerai tu?

GILDA

E voi?

DUCA

L'intera vita . . . poi . . .

GILDA

Non più . . . non più . . . partite.

GILDA, DUCA

Addio, speranza ed anima
Sol tu sarai per me.
Addio, vivrà immutabile
L'affetto mio per te.

*(Il Duca esce scortato da Giovanna, Gilda
resta fissando la porta ond'è partito)*

GILDA

Gualtier Maldè . . . nome di lui sì
amato,
Ti scolpisci nel cor innamorato.

Caro nome che'l mio cor
Festi primo palpitar,
Le delizie dell'amor
Mi dèi sempre rammentar!

DUKE

(To himself)

Ah, if I could
Catch the traitor
Who disturbs me!

GILDA

(To Giovanna)

Show him out by the terrace.
Go now.

DUKE

Tell me, will you love me?

GILDA

And you?

DUKE

My whole life . . . then . . .

GILDA

No more . . . no more . . . go now.

GILDA AND DUKE

Farewell, farewell, my hope and my soul
You will always be.
Farewell, my feeling for you
Will live forever.

*(The Duke leaves, escorted by Giovanna. Gilda
remains, gazing at the door through which he has left)*

GILDA

Walter Maldé . . . the name of him I
love so much,
You are engraved on my enamoured heart.

Dearest name which first
Made my heart tremble,
You will always recall
The delights of love to me.

Col pensier il mio desir
A te sempre volerà,
E fin l'ultimo sospir,
Caro nome, tuo sarà.

(Sale al terrazzo con una lanterna)

*(Marullo, Ceprano, Borsa, Cortigiani, armati
e mascherati, entrano nella via. Sul terrazzo
Gilda che tosto entra in casa)*

BORSA

(indicando Gilda al Coro)

È là.

CONTE DI CEPRANO

Miratela.

CORO

Oh, quanto è bella!

MARULLO

Par fata od angiol.

CORO

L'amante è quella
Di Rigoletto.

(Rigoletto viene per la via, concentrato)

RIGOLETTO

(tra sé)

Riedo! perché?

BORSA

Silenzio, all'opra, badate a me.

RIGOLETTO

(tra sé)

Ah, da quel vecchio fui maledetto!

(Urta in Borsa, forte:)

With my thoughts, my desire
Will always fly to you,
And my last breath
Will utter your dear name.

(Ascends to the terrace with a lantern)

*(Marullo, Ceprano, Borsa and the courtiers,
armed and masked, appear in the street. On
the terrace, Gilda is about to enter the house)*

BORSA

(Indicating Gilda to the Chorus)

There she is.

COUNT CEPRANO

Look at her.

CHORUS

Oh, how beautiful she is.

MARULLO

Like a fairy or an angel.

CHORUS

That is the mistress of
Rigoletto.

(Rigoletto returns, in deep thought)

RIGOLETTO

(To himself)

I've come back. Why?

BORSA

Silence, to work now, follow me.

RIGOLETTO

(To himself)

Oh, I was cursed by that old man!

(Stumbles against Borsa. Aloud:)

Chi va là?

Who's there.

BORSA

BORSA

(ai compagni)

(To his companions)

Tacete, c'è Rigoletto.

Quiet, it's Rigoletto.

CONTE DI CEPRANO

COUNT CEPRANO

Vittoria doppia! L'uccideremo.

A double victory. Let's kill him.

BORSA

BORSA

No, chè domani più rideremo.

No, we'll have a better laugh tomorrow.

MARULLO

MARULLO

Or tutto aggiusto.

Now I'll arrange everything.

RIGOLETTO

RIGOLETTO

Chi parla qua?

Who's talking?

MARULLO

MARULLO

Ehi, Rigoletto? Di'?

Eh, Rigoletto, Tell me—

RIGOLETTO

RIGOLETTO

(con voce terribile)

(In a fierce voice)

Chi va là?

Who is it?

MARULLO

MARULLO

Eh, non mangiarci! Son . . .

Eh, don't eat us. It's . . .

RIGOLETTO

RIGOLETTO

Chi?

Who?

MARULLO

MARULLO

Marullo.

Marullo.

RIGOLETTO

RIGOLETTO

In tanto buio lo sguardo è nullo.

It's so dark, I can't see anything.

MARULLO

MARULLO

Qui ne condusse ridevol cosa . . .
Tôrre a Ceprano vogliam la sposa . . .

A joke of ours has brought us here . . .
We want to abduct Ceprano's wife . . .

RIGOLETTO

(tra sé)

Ahimè! respiro!

(forte)

Ma come entrare?

MARULLO

(a Ceprano)

La vostra chiave?

(a Rigoletto)

Non dubitare.
Non dee mancarci lo stratagemma.

(Gli dà la chiave avuta da Ceprano)

Ecco la chiave.

RIGOLETTO

(palpando)

Sento il suo stemma.

(tra sé)

Ah, terror vano fu dunque il mio!

(respirando)

N'è là il palazzo. Con voi son io.

MARULLO

Siam mascherati.

RIGOLETTO

Ch'io pur mi mascheri!
A me una larva.

MARULLO

Sì, pronta è già.

*(Gli mette una maschera e nello stesso tempo
lo benda con un fazzoletto, e lo pone a reggere
una scala, che avranno appostata al
terrazzo)*

RIGOLETTO

(To himself)

Thank heavens, I can breathe again!

(Aloud)

But how will you get in?

MARULLO

(To Ceprano)

Give me your key.

(To Rigoletto)

Have no doubts,
Our plan can't fail.

(He gives Rigoletto the key taken from Ceprano)

Here's the key.

RIGOLETTO

(Feeling it)

I can feel his crest.

(To himself)

Ah, my fears, then, were unfounded.

(He breathes freely)

There's his palace. I'll come with you.

MARULLO

We're masked.

RIGOLETTO

I'll wear a mask, too.
Give me one.

MARULLO

Here's one for you.

*(Puts a mask on him and at the same time
ties a handkerchief over his eyes, then gets him
to hold a ladder which they have placed
against the terrace)*

Terrai la scala.

Hold the ladder.

RIGOLETTO

Fitta è la tenebra.

RIGOLETTO

It's completely dark.

MARULLO

(ai compagni)

La benda cieco e sordo il fa.

MARULLO

(To his companions)

The bandage will make him blind and deaf.

TUTTI

Zitti, zitti, moviamo a vendetta;
Ne sia côlto or che meno l'aspetta.
Derisore sì audace, costante,
A sua volta schernito sarà!
Cheti, cheti, rubiamgli l'amante
E la Corte doman riderà.

ALL

Softy, softly, now for vengeance;
We'll strike now when he least expects it.
The ever audacious scoffer
Shall in his turn be scoffed at!
Quiet, quiet, we'll steal his mistress,
And tomorrow the Court will have a laugh.

(Alcuni salgono al terrazzo, rompono la porta del primo piano, scendono, aprono ad altri che entrano dalla strada e riescono trascinando Gilda, la quale avrà la bocca chiusa da un fazzoletto. Nel traversare la scena ella perde una sciarpa)

(A few climb to the terrace, force open the door to the first floor, then come down to open the gate for the others who enter from the street. They come out again, dragging Gilda, who is gagged with a handkerchief. As she is being borne across the stage, she loses her scarf)

GILDA

(da lontano)

Soccorso, padre mio!

GILDA

(From the distance)

Help, father!

CORO

Vittoria!

CHORUS

Victory!

GILDA

(più lontano)

Aita!

GILDA

(Further away)

Help!

RIGOLETTO

Non han finito ancor! Qual derisione!

(Si tocca gli occhi)

Sono bendato!
Oh, Gilda!

RIGOLETTO

Haven't they finished yet? What nonsense.

(Puts his hand to his eyes)

I'm blindfolded.
Oh, Gilda!

(Si strappa impetuosamente la benda e la maschera, ed al chiarore d'una lanterna scordata riconosce la sciarpa, vede la porta aperta; entra, ne trae Giovanna spaventata; la fissa con istupore, si strappa i capelli senza poter gridare; finalmente, dopo molti sforzi, esclama:)

Ah! la maledizione!

(sviene)

(Impetuously, he tears off blindfold and mask, sees the scarf by the light of a lantern, also the open door. He enters, and drags out a terrified Giovanna, gazes at her dully, and tears his hair without making a sound. Finally, after much effort, he exclaims:)

Ah, the curse!

(He faints)

ATTO SECONDO

*Salotto nel Palazzo Ducale. Vi sono due
porte laterali, una maggiore nel fondo che si
schiude. Ai suoi lati pendono i ritratti, in
tutta figura, a sinistra del Duca, a destra
della sua sposa. V'ha un seggiolone presso
una tavola coperta di velluto e altri mobili.*

DUCA

(agitato)

Ella mi fu rapita!
E quando, o ciel? Ne' brevi
Istanti prima che il mio presagio interno
Sull'orma corsa ancora mi spingesse!
Schiuso era l'uscio! E la magion
deserta!
E dove ora sarà quell'angiol caro?
Colei che prima potè in questo core
Destar la fiamma di costanti affetti?

Colei sì pura, al cui modesto sguardo
Quasi spinto a virtù talor mi credo!
Ella mi fu rapita!
E chi l'ardiva?
Ma ne avrò vendetta.
Lo chiede il pianto della mia diletta.
Parmi veder le lagrime
Scorrenti da quel ciglio,
Quando fra il dubbio e l'ansia
Del sùbito periglio,
Dell'amor nostro memore
Il suo Gualtier chiamò.
Ned ei potea soccorrerti,
Cara fanciulla amata;
Ei che vorria coll'anima
Farti quaggiù beata;
Ei che le sfere agli angeli
Per te non invidiò.

*(Marullo, Conte di Ceprano, Borsa ed altri
Cortigiani, entranno)*

TUTTI

Duca, duca?

ACT II

*A salon in the ducal palace. Two side doors,
and a larger door at the back, with full-length
portraits hanging on either side: on the left
the Duke, on the right his wife. A large
chair near a table covered in velvet, and other
furniture.*

DUKE

(agitated)

She has been stolen from me!
But when, oh heaven? Only a few
Moments before some inner foreboding
Led me to retrace my steps!
The door was open, and the house
deserted!
And where is that beloved angel now?
She, the first who was able to awaken in
my heart
The flame of constant love.
She, so pure, whose modest glance
Almost makes me believe myself virtuous.
She has been stolen from me!
Who has dared to do it?
I shall have vengeance on him;
The tears of my beloved demand it.
I seem to see the tears
Flowing from her eyes,
When, torn between doubt and fear
At this sudden danger,
remembering our love
She called for her Walter.
He could not help you,
dearly loved maiden,
He who would give his soul
To make you happy here on earth,
He who, because of you,
Did not even envy the angels in their spheres.

*(Marullo, Ceprano, Borsa and other
Courtiers enter)*

ALL

My lord, my lord.

DUCA	**DUKE**
Ebben?	Well?
TUTTI	**ALL**
L'amante Fu rapita a Rigoletto.	We've kidnapped Rigoletto's mistress.
DUCA	**DUKE**
Come! E d'onde?	What? Where from?
TUTTI	**ALL**
Dal suo tetto.	From his house.
DUCA	**DUKE**
Ah! ah! Dite, come fu?	Ha, ha! Tell me, how did it happen?
(siede)	*(He sits)*
TUTTI	**ALL**
Scorrendo uniti in remota via, Brev'ora dopo caduto il dì, Come previsto ben s'era in pria, Rara beltà ci si scoprì. Era l'amante di Rigoletto, Che vista appena si dileguò. Già di rapirla s'avea il progetto, Quando il buffone vêr noi spuntò; Che di Ceprano noi la contessa Rapir volessimo, stolto, credè; La scala, quindi, all'uopo messa, Bendato ei stesso ferma tenè. Salimmo e rapidi la giovinetta A noi riusciva quindi asportar. Quand'ei s'accorse della vendetta Restò scornato ad imprecar.	Going along a remote street together, Shortly after sunset, As we'd arranged earlier in the evening, We discovered a rare beauty. It was Rigoletto's mistress, Who vanished immediately we'd seen her. We'd already planned to abduct her When the jester came towards us; He foolishly beleived that we wanted To carry off the Countess Ceprano; The ladder we'd set up He himself held for us, blindfolded. We climbed up, seized the girl Quickly, and carried her off. When he realized how we'd had our revenge, He stood there, shamed and cursing.
DUCA	**DUKE**
(tra sé)	*(To himself)*
O cielo! È dessa! La mia diletta!	Heavens! It's she, my beloved.
(al Coro)	*(To the Chorus)*
Ma dove or trovasi la poveretta?	But where's the poor girl now?

TUTTI	ALL
Fu da noi stessi addotta or qui.	We brought her here ourselves.
DUCA	DUKE
(tra sé)	*(To himself)*
Ah, tutto il cielo non mi rapì!	Ah, heaven has not taken everything from me.
(alzandosi con gioia)	*(Rising, joyously)*
Possente amor mi chiama,	Powerful love calls me,
Volar io deggio a lei:	And I must fly to her:
Il serto mio darei	I would give my crown
Per consolar quel cor.	To console her heart.
Ah! sappia alfin chi l'ama,	Ah, at last she shall know who loves her,
Conosca alfin chi sono,	At last learn who I am.
Apprenda ch'anco in trono	She shall discover that even rulers
Ha degli schiavi Amor.	Can be the slaves of love.
(Esce frettoloso dal mezzo.)	*(Rushes out through the centre door)*
TUTTI	ALL
Oh! Qual pensier or l'agita?	Oh, what thought now agitates him?
Come cangiò d'umor!	How his mood has changed!
(Rigoletto entra cantarellando con represso dolore)	*(Rigoletto enters, singing with repressed sadness)*
MARULLO	MARULLO
Povero Rigoletto!	Poor Rigoletto.
RIGOLETTO	RIGOLETTO
La rà la là.	Lara, Lala
CORO	CHORUS
Ei vien! Silenzio.	He's coming. Silence.
TUTTI	ALL
Buon giorno, Rigoletto!	Good day, Rigoletto.
RIGOLETTO	RIGOLETTO
(tra sé)	*(To himself)*
Han tutti fatto il colpo!	They were all part of it.

CONTE DI CEPRANO

Ch'hai di nuovo, buffon?

RIGOLETTO

Ch'hai di nuovo, buffon?
Che dell'usato
Più noioso voi siete.

TUTTI

Ah! ah! ah! ah!

RIGOLETTO

(spiando inquieto dovunque, tra sé)

Ove l'avran nascosta?

TUTTI

(piano)

Guardate com'è inquieto!

RIGOLETTO

(a Marullo)

Son felice
Che nulla a voi nuocesse
L'aria di questa notte!

MARULLO

Questa notte!

RIGOLETTO

Sì, ah, fu il bel colpo!

MARULLO

S'ho dormito sempre!

RIGOLETTO

Ah, voi dormiste! Avrò dunque
sognato!

(S'allontana e vedendo un fazzoletto sopra una tavola ne osserva inquieto la cifra)

COUNT CEPRANO

What news, jester?

RIGOLETTO

What news, jester?
That you're all
More tedious than ever.

ALL

Ha, ha, ha, ha!

RIGOLETTO

(To himself, anxiously searching everywhere)

Where have they hidden her?

ALL

(Softly)

See how anxious he is!

RIGOLETTO

(To Marullo)

I'm delighted
To see that you have not suffered
From the night air, last night.

MARULLO

Last night?

RIGOLETTO

Yes. Ah, it was a beautiful joke.

MARULLO

I slept the whole night through.

RIGOLETTO

Ah, you slept! Then I was dreaming!

(Walks away, and, seeing a handkerchief on a table, anxiously examines it)

TUTTI	ALL
(piano)	*(Softly)*
Ve' come tutto osserva!	See how he looks at everything.
RIGOLETTO	RIGOLETTO
(gettandolo, tra sé)	*(To himself, throwing the handkerchief away)*
Non è il suo.	It's not hers.
(forte)	*(Aloud)*
Dorme il Duca tuttor?	Is the Duke still asleep?
TUTTI	ALL
Sì, dorme ancora.	Yes, he's still asleep.
(Un Paggio della Duchessa entra)	*(A page of the Duchess enters)*
PAGGIO	PAGE
Al suo sposo parlar vuol la Duchessa.	The Duchess wishes to speak to her husband.
CONTE DI CEPRANO	COUNT CEPRANO
Dorme.	He's asleep.
PAGGIO	PAGE
Qui or or con voi non era?	Was he not with you just now?
BORSA	BORSA
È a caccia.	He's gone hunting.
PAGGIO	PAGE
Senza paggi! senz'armi!	Without pages? Unarmed?
TUTTI	ALL
E non capisci	Don't you understand
Che per ora vedere non può alcuno?	That at present he doesn't want to see anyone?
RIGOLETTO	RIGOLETTO
(che a parte è stato attentissimo al dialogo, balzando improvvisamente tra loro prorompe:)	*(Who has been standing aside, listening, suddenly leaps forward, crying out:)*
Ah, ell'è qui dunque! Ell'è col Duca!	Ah, then she's here. She's with the Duke!

TUTTI	ALL
Chi?	Who?
RIGOLETTO	RIGOLETTO
La giovin che stanotte	The girl whom, last night,
Al mio tetto rapiste.	You abducted from my house.
Ma la saprò riprender.	But I shall have her back.
Ella è là!	She is here.
TUTTI	ALL
Se l'amante perdesti, la ricerca	If you've lost your mistress, she's been
Altrove.	found by someone else
RIGOLETTO	RIGOLETTO
Io vo' mia figlia!	I want my daughter!
TUTTI	ALL
La sua figlia!	His daughter!
RIGOLETTO	RIGOLETTO
Sì, la mia figlia! d'una tal vittoria	Yes, my daughter. Such a victory,
Che, adesso non ridete?	Doesn't it make you laugh?
Ella è là. La voglio, la renderete.	She is here. I want her. Give her back to me.
(Corre verso la porta di mezzo, ma i	(Rushes to the centre door, but the Courtiers
Cortigiani gli attraversano il passaggio)	block his way)
Cortigiani, vil razza dannata,	Courtiers, vile, damned race,
Per qual prezzo vendeste il mio bene?	For what price have you sold my dear girl?
A voi nulla per l'oro sconviene,	To you, nothing is worth more than money,
Ma mia figlia è impagabil tesor.	But my daughter is a treasure beyond price.
La rendete . . . o, se pur disarmata,	Give her back . . . or, even though I
Questa man per voi fora cruenta;	carry no weapons,
Nulla in terra più l'uomo paventa,	My hands will strike you down;
Se dei figli difende l'onor.	He fears nothing more on earth
Quella porta, assassini, m'aprite.	Who defends his child's honour.
	Let me through that door, assassins.
(Si getta ancora sulla porta che gli è	(Again he throws himself against the door,
nuovamente contesa dai Gentiluomini; lotta	and is stopped by the Courtiers. He struggles
alquanto, poi ritorna spossato sul davanti	briefly, then returns wearily to the front of the
della scena)	stage)
Ah! Voi tutti a me contro venite!	Ah, you are all against me!

(piange)

Ebbene, piango, Marullo . . . signore,
Tu ch'hai l'alma gentil come il core,
Dimmi tu dove l'hanno nascosta?
È là? . . . Non è vero? . . . Tu taci,
ohimé?
Miei signori, perdono, pietate,
Al vegliardo la figlia ridate.
Riconarla a voi nulla ora costa,
Tutto al mondo è tal figlia per me.
Pietà, signori, pietà!

*(Gilda esce dalla stanza a sinistra e
si getta nelle paterne braccia)*

GILDA

Mio padre!

RIGOLETTO

Dio! Mia Gilda!
Signori, in essa è tutta
La mia famiglia. Non temer più nulla,
Angelo mio.

(ai Cortigiani)

Fu scherzo, non è vero?
Io, che pur piansi, or rido.
E tu perché piangi?

GILDA

Ah, l'onta, padre mio!

RIGOLETTO

Cielo! Che dici?

GILDA

Arrossir voglio innanzi a voi soltanto.

RIGOLETTO

Ite di qua voi tutti.
Se il duca vostro d'appressarsi osasse,
Che non entri, gli dite, e qui io sono.

(Weeps)

Well then, I am weeping. Marullo . . . my lord,
You who are both kind-hearted and noble,
Tell me where they have hidden her.
Is she there? . . . Isn't it so? . . . You're
silent, alas!
My lords, forgive me, have pity,
Give an old man back his daughter.
To give her back costs you nothing now,
And my daughter is all the world to me.
Pity, pity, my lords, have pity!

*(Gilda enters from the room on the left, and
throws herself into her father's arms)*

GILDA

My father!

RIGOLETTO

God! My Gilda,
Sirs, she is all
My family. Don't be frightened any more,
My angel.

(To the Courtiers)

It was a joke, wasn't it?
I, who was weeping, laugh now.
Why do you weep?

GILDA

Ah, the shame, my father.

RIGOLETTO

Heavens! What are you saying?

GILDA

Let my blushes be seen by you alone.

RIGOLETTO

Away with you all.
If your Duke should dare to approach,
Tell him not to enter, for I am here.

(Si abbandona sul seggiolone)

TUTTI

(fra loro)

Coi fanciulli e coi dementi
Spesso giova il simular;
Partiam pur, ma quel ch'ei tenti
Non lasciamo d'osservar.

(Escono dal mezzo e chiudono la porta)

RIGOLETTO

Parla, siam soli.

GILDA

(tra sé)

Ciel! dammi coraggio!

(forte)

Tutte le feste al tempio
Mentre pregava Iddio,
Bello e fatale un giovane
Offriasi al guardo mio.
Se i labbri nostri tacquero
Dagli occhi il cor parlò.
Furtivo fra le tenebre
Sol ieri a me giungeva.
Sono studente, povero,
Commosso, mi diceva,
E con ardente palpito
Amor mi protestò.
Partì. Il mio core aprivasi
A speme più gradita,
Quando improvvisi apparvero
Color che m'han rapita.
E a forza qui m'addussero
Nell'ansia più crudel.

RIGOLETTO

(tra sé)

Ah! Solo per me l'infamia
A te chiedeva, o Dio,
Ch'ella potesse ascendere
Quanto caduto er'io.

(He sits in the big chair)

ALL

(To themselves)

With children and madmen,
It's often best to pretend;
Let's go then, but keep watch
To see what he does.

(They leave through the centre door, and close it)

RIGOLETTO

Speak, we are alone.

GILDA

(To herself)

Heaven give me courage.

(Aloud)

Every Sunday in church
While I was praying to God,
A fatally handsome young man
Would present himself to my view.
Though our lips were silent,
Through our eyes our hearts spoke.
Secretly in the darkness
Last night he visited me.
I am a student, and poor,
He told me in great emotion,
And with ardently beating heart
Protested his love for me.
He left. My heart aspired
To hopes of bliss,
When suddenly there appeared
Those men who abducted me,
And by force brought me here
In most cruel anguish.

RIGOLETTO

(To himself)

Ah, infamy for myself alone
I begged from you, oh God,
That she might rise
As much as I had fallen.

Ah, presso del patibolo
Bisogna ben l'altare!
Ma tutto ora scompare,
L'altare si rovesciò!

(forte)

Ah! Piangi, fanciulla, e scorrer
Fa il pianto sul mio cor.

GILDA

Padre, in voi parla un angelo
Per me consolator.

RIGOLETTO

Compiuto pur quanto a fare mi resta
Lasciare potremo quest'aura funesta.

GILDA

Sì.

RIGOLETTO

E tutto un sol giorno cangiare potè!

*(Entra un Usciere e il Conte di Monterone,
che dalla destra attraversa il fondo della
sala fra gli alabardieri)*

USCIERE

(alle Guardie)

Schiudete, ire al carcere Monteron de'.

CONTE DI MONTERONE

(fermandosi verso il ritratto del Duca)

Poichè fosti invano da me maledetto,
Nè un fulmine o un ferro colpiva il tuo
petto,
Felice pur anco, o duca, vivrai.

(Esce fra le Guardie dal mezzo)

Ah, close to the gallows
There is most need of the altar!
But now everything is crumbling,
The altar is overthrown!

(Aloud)

Ah, weep, my child, and let
Your tears fall on my heart.

GILDA

Father, in you there speaks an angel
To console me.

RIGOLETTO

Once I've done what remains for me to do,
We can leave this baleful place.

GILDA

Yes.

RIGOLETTO

That everything could be so changed in
a single day.

*(An usher enters, followed by Count
Monterone between halberdiers. They cross the
back of the hall from the right)*

USHER

(To the guards)

Make way, Monterone is being taken to prison.

COUNT MONTERONE

(Stopping before the portrait of the Duke)

Since I cursed you in vain,
And neither lightning nor sword has
struck your breast,
Live on happily, oh Duke.

(Exit through the centre, with the guards)

RIGOLETTO

No, vecchio, t'inganni, un vindice avrai.

(con impeto, volto al ritratto)

Sì, vendetta, tremenda vendetta
Di quest'anima è solo desio,
Di punirti già l'ora s'affretta,
Che fatale per te suonerà.
Come fulmin scagliato da Dio
Te colpire il buffone saprà.

GILDA

O mio padre, qual gioia feroce
Balenarvi negli occhi vegg'io!
Perdonate . . . a noi pure una voce
Di perdono dal cielo verrà.

(tra sé)

Mi tradiva, pur l'amo; gran Dio,
Per l'ingrato ti chiedo pietà!

(escono)

RIGOLETTO

No, old man, you are mistaken. You
shall have an avenger.

(With vehemence, turning to the portrait)

Yes, revenge, dire revenge,
Is the sole desire of my heart.
The hour of punishment approaches
That will sound fatally for you.
Like a thunderbolt hurled by God,
The jester knows how to strike you.

GILDA

Oh father, what ferocious joy
I see flashing in your eyes!
Forgive him . . . just as for us a voice
From heaven will call for pardon.

(To herself)

He betrayed me, but I love him; Oh God,
I ask for pity for the unworthy man.

(Exeunt)

ATTO TERZO

La sponda destra del Mincio. A sinistra è una casa a due piani, mezzo diroccata, la cui fronte, volta allo spettatore, lascia vedere per una grande arcata l'interno d'una rustica osteria al pian terreno, ed una rozza scala che mette al granaio, entro cui, da un balcone senza imposte, si vede un lettuccio. Nella facciata che guarda la strada è una porta che s'apre per di dentro; il muro poi è sì pieno di fessure, che dal di fuori si può facilmente scorgere quanto avviene nell'interno. Il resto del teatro rappresenta la deserta parte del Mincio, che nel fondo scorre dietro un parapetto in mezza ruina; di là dal fiume è Mantova. È notte.

Gilda e Rigoletto inquieti, sono sulla strada. Sparafucile nell'interno dell'osteria, seduto presso una tavola, sta ripulendo il suo cinturone senza nulla intendere di quanto accade al di fuori.

RIGOLETTO

E l'ami?

GILDA

Sempre.

RIGOLETTO

Pure tempo a guarine t'ho lasciato.

GILDA

Io l'amo.

RIGOLETTO

Povero cor di donna! Ah, il vile infame!
Ma ne avrai vendetta, o Gilda.

GILDA

Pietà, mio padre.

ACT III

The right bank of the river Mincio. On the left is a two-storied house, half in ruins, through whose front one can see, behind a large archway, the inside of a rustic inn on the ground floor, and a rough staircase leading to a loft in which, through an open balcony, a couch can be seen. Fronting on the street is a door which opens from within. The wall is so full of cracks that one can easily see in from the outside. The rest of the scene represents the deserted area around the Mincio, which, at the back, flows behind a half-ruined parapet. Beyond the river lies Mantua. It is night.

Gilda and Rigoletto, looking anxious, are in the street. Sparafucile is inside the inn, seated by a table, polishing his belt. He can hear nothing of what happens outside.

RIGOLETTO

So you love him?

GILDA

For ever.

RIGOLETTO

Yet I have given you time to get over it.

GILDA

I love him.

RIGOLETTO

Poor heart of woman! Ah, the vile wretch!
But you shall be avenged, oh Gilda.

GILDA

Have pity, my father.

RIGOLETTO

E se tu certa fossi
Ch'ei ti tradisse, l'ameresti ancora?

GILDA

Non so, ma pur m'adora.

RIGOLETTO

Egli?

GILDA

Sì.

RIGOLETTO

Ebbene, osserva dunque.

(La conduce presso una delle fessure del muro, ed ella vi guarda)

GILDA

Un uomo vedo.

RIGOLETTO

Per poco attendi.

(Il Duca, in assisa di semplice ufficiale di cavalleria, entra nella sala terrena per una porta a sinistra)

GILDA

(trasalendo)

Ah, padre mio!

DUCA

(a Sparafucile)

Due cose e tosto.

SPARAFUCILE

Quali?

DUCA

Una stanza e del vino.

RIGOLETTO

But if you were certain
That he'd betrayed you, would you love him still?

GILDA

I don't know, but still he adores me.

RIGOLETTO

He?

GILDA

Yes.

RIGOLETTO

Well then, take a look.

(He leads her to a crack in the wall, and she looks in)

GILDA

I see a man.

RIGOLETTO

Wait a little.

(Dressed in the simple uniform of a cavalry officer, the Duke enters by a door on the left)

GILDA

(Surprised)

Ah, father!

DUKE

(To Sparafucile)

Two things, and quickly.

SPARAFUCILE

What are they?

DUKE

A room and some wine.

RIGOLETTO

(piano)

Son questi i suoi costumi!

SPARAFUCILE

(tra sé)

Oh, il bel zerbino!

(Entra nella stanza vicina)

DUCA

La donna è mobile
Qual piuma al vento,
Muta d'accento
E di pensiero.
Sempre un amabile
Leggiadro viso,
In pianto o in riso,
È menzognero.

È sempre misero
Chi a lei s'affida,
Chi le confida,
Mal cauto il core!
Pur mai non sentesi
Felice appieno
Chi sul quel seno,
Non liba amore!

SPARAFUCILE

(Rientra con una bottiglia di vino e due
bicchieri che depone sulla tavola; quindi batte
col pomo della sua lunga spada due colpi al
soffitto. A quel segnale una ridente giovane, in
costume di zingara, scende a salti la scala. Il
Duca corre per abbracciarla, ma ella gli
sfugge. Frattanto Sparafucile, uscito sulla
via, dice a parte a Rigoletto:)

È là il vostr'uomo. Viver de' o morire?

RIGOLETTO

Più tardi tornerò l'opra a compire.

(Sparafucile si allontana dietro la casa verso
il fiume)

RIGOLETTO

(Softly)

These are his habits.

SPARAFUCILE

(To himself)

Oh, the fine dandy.

(Goes into the next room)

DUKE

Woman is as wayward
As a feather in the wind,
Changeable in word
And in thought.
Always a pleasant
Smiling face,
But, whether crying or laughing,
Deceitful.

Continually wretched
Is he who trusts her;
He who confides in her
Has his heart broken!
But no man can be
Completely happy
If from her breast
He has never sipped love.

SPARAFUCILE

(Returns with a bottle of wine and two
glasses which he puts on the table; he then
knocks twice on the ceiling with his sword.
At this signal, a smiling young woman,
dressed as a gypsy, runs down the staircase.
The Duke rushes to embrace her, but she
avoids him. Meanwhile, Sparafucile has gone
out into the street and says, aside, to Rigoletto:)

Your man is there. Shall he live or die?

RIGOLETTO

I'll come back later to make a decision.

(Sparafucile goes behind the house towards
the river)

DUCA

Un dì, se ben rammentomi,
O bella, t'incontrai.
Mi piacque di te chiedere
E intesi che qui stai.
Or sappi che d'allora
Sol te quest'alma adora.

GILDA

Iniquo!

MADDALENA

Ah! ah! e vent'altre appresso
Le scorda forse adesso?
Ha un'aria il signorino
Da vero libertino.

DUCA

Sì, un mostro son.

(per abbracciarla)

MADDALENA

Lasciatemi, stordito.

DUCA

Ih, che fracasso!

MADDALENA

Stia saggio.

DUCA

E tu sii docile,
Non farmi tanto chiasso.
Ogni saggezza chiudesi
Nel gaudio e nell'amore.

(Le prende la mano)

La bella mano candida!

MADDALENA

Scherzate voi, signore.

DUKE

One day, as I remember well,
Oh beautiful one, I met you.
It pleased me to seek you out,
And I discovered you lived here.
You know that, since then,
My heart has adored you alone.

GILDA

Wicked man!

MADDALENA

Ha, ha, but the twenty others
You've addressed thus, you're forgetting.
The young gentleman has the air
Of a real libertine.

DUKE

Yes, I'm a monster.

(He goes to embrace her)

MADDALENA

Let me go, you're too bold.

DUKE

Oh, what a fuss.

MADDALENA

Be prudent.

DUKE

And you, be docile,
And don't make such a fuss.
Let's forget prudence
And enjoy the delights of love.

(He takes her hand)

Such a beautiful white hand!

MADDALENA

You're joking, sir.

DUCA

No, no.

MADDALENA

Son brutta.

DUCA

Abbracciami.

GILDA

Iniquo!

MADDALENA

Ebbro!

DUCA

D'amore ardente.

MADDALENA

Signor, l'indifferente
Vi piace canzonar?

DUCA

No, no, ti vo' sposar.

MADDALENA

Ne voglio la parola.

DUCA

(ironico)

Amabile figliuola!

RIGOLETTO

(a Gilda che avrà tutto osservato ed inteso)

E non ti basta ancor?

GILDA

Iniquo traditor!

DUKE

No, no.

MADDALENA

I'm ugly.

DUKE

Embrace me.

GILDA

Wicked man!

MADDALENA

You're drunk!

DUKE

With ardent love.

MADDALENA

Indifferent sire,
It pleases you to jest?

DUKE

No, no, I want to marry you.

MADDALENA

I want your word on that.

DUKE

(Ironically)

Sweet little girl!

RIGOLETTO

(To Gilda, who has seen and heard
everything)

Is this not enough for you?

GILDA

Wicked traitor!

DUCA

Bella figlia dell'amore,
Schiavo son de' vezzi tuoi;
Con un detto sol tu puoi
Le mie pene consolar.
Vieni e senti del mio core
Il frequente palpitar.

MADDALENA

Ah! ah! Rido ben di core,
Chè tai baie costan poco;
Quanto valga il vostro gioco,
Mel credete, so apprezzar.
Sono avvezza, bel signore,
Ad un simile scherzar.

GILDA

Ah, così parlar d'amore
A me pur l'infame ho udito!
Infelice cor tradito,
Per angoscia non scoppiar.
Perché, o credulo mio core,
Un tal uom dovevi amar?

RIGOLETTO

(a Gilda)

Taci, il pianger non vale;
Ch'ei mentiva or sei sicura.
Taci, e mia sarà la cura
La vendetta d'affrettar.
Pronta fia. sarà fatale;
Io saprollo fulminar.
M'odi, ritorna a casa.
Oro prendi, un destriero,
Una veste viril che t'apprestai,
E per Verona parti.
Sarovvi io pur domani.

GILDA

Or venite.

RIGOLETTO

Impossibil.

DUKE

Beautiful daughter of love,
I am the slave of your charms;
With a single word you can
Comfort my sorrows.
Come and feel how my heart
Beats swiftly.

MADDALENA

Ha, ha, I laugh with all my heart,
For such flattery costs little;
How much your game is worth,
I understand, believe me.
I'm accustomed, my handsome gentleman,
To jests of this kind.

GILDA

Ah, words of love like this
I too heard from this infamous man!
Unhappy betrayed heart,
Do not break in your anguish.
Why, oh credulous heart of mine,
Did you have to love such a man?

RIGOLETTO

(To Gilda)

Quiet, your weeping is useless;
Now you are convinced he was lying.
Be quiet. Mine be the task
Of exacting vengeance.
Let it be soon, and fatal.
I shall strike him down.
Listen to me! Return home,
Take money, a horse, and
A man's cloak I've left out for you,
And leave for Verona.
I shall join you there tomorrow.

GILDA

Come now.

RIGOLETTO

Impossible.

GILDA

Tremo.

RIGOLETTO

Va.

(Gilda parte. Durante questa scena e la
seguente il Duca e Maddalena stanno fra loro
parlando, ridendo, bevendo. Partita Gilda,
Rigoletto va dietro la casa, e ritorna parlando
con Sparafucile e contandogli delle monete)

RIGOLETTO

Venti scudi hai tu detto?
Eccone dieci,
E dopo l'opra il resto.
Ei qui rimane?

SPARAFUCILE

Sì.

RIGOLETTO

Alla mezzanotte ritornerò.

SPARAFUCILE

Non cale;
A gettarlo nel fiume basto io solo.

RIGOLETTO

No, no; il vo' far io stesso.

SPARAFUCILE

Sia! Il suo nome?

RIGOLETTO

Vuoi saper anche il mio?
Egli è «Delitto», «Punizion» son io.

(Parte. Il cielo si oscura e tuona)

GILDA

I tremble.

RIGOLETTO

Go.

(Gilda leaves. During this dialogue and the
next, the Duke and Maddalena are seen to be
talking, laughing and drinking. When Gilda
has gone, Rigoletto goes behind the house and
returns talking to Sparafucile, to whom he
counts out money)

RIGOLETTO

Twenty scudi, you said?
Here's ten,
And the rest when you've finished the job.
Is he staying here?

SPARAFUCILE

Yes.

RIGOLETTO

I'll return at midnight.

SPARAFUCILE

There's no need;
I can throw him into the river alone.

RIGOLETTO

No, no, I want to do that myself.

SPARAFUCILE

Very well. What is his name?

RIGOLETTO

Do you want to know mine as well?
He is 'Crime', I am 'Punishment'.

(They leave. The sky becomes dark. Thunder
and lightning are heard)

SPARAFUCILE

La tempesta è vicina!
Più scura fia la notte.

DUCA

Maddalena!

(per prenderla)

MADDALENA

(sfuggendogli)

Aspettate, mio fratello viene.

DUCA

Che importa?

(S'ode il tuono)

MADDALENA

Tuona!

SPARAFUCILE

(entrando)

E pioverà fra poco.

DUCA

Tanto meglio,
Tu dormirai in scuderia,
All'inferno . . . ove vorrai.

SPARAFUCILE

Oh! Grazie.

MADDALENA

(piano al Duca)

Ah no! partite.

DUCA

(a Maddalena)

Con tal tempo?

SPARAFUCILE

The storm is getting close,
And the night grows darker.

DUKE

Maddalena!

(Trying to catch her)

MADDALENA

(Escaping him)

Wait, my brother's coming.

DUKE

What does that matter?

(Thunder is heard)

MADDALENA

Thunder!

SPARAFUCILE

(As he enters)

It will soon start raining.

DUKE

All the better;
You can sleep in the stable,
In hell . . . or wherever you like.

SPARAFUCILE

Oh, thank you.

MADDALENA

(Softly, to the Duke)

Ah no, please go.

DUKE

(To Maddalena)

In this weather?

SPARAFUCILE

(piano a Maddalena)

Son venti scudi d'oro.

(al Duca)

Ben felice d'offrirvi la mia stanza.
Se a voi piace
Tosto a vederla andiamo.

(Prende un lume e s'avvia per la scala)

DUCA

Ebben, sono con te, presto, vediamo.

*(Dice una parola all'orecchio di Maddalena e
segue Sparafucile)*

MADDALENA

Povero giovin, grazïoso tanto!
Dio, qual notte è questa!

DUCA

*(giunto al granaio, vedendone il balcone senza
imposte)*

Si dorme all'aria aperta? bene, bene!
Buona notte.

SPARAFUCILE

Signor, vi guardi Iddio!

DUCA

Breve sonno dormiam; stanco son io.

La donna è mobile
Qual piuma al vento . . .

*(Depone il capello, la spada, e si stende sul
letto, dove in breve s'addormenta. Maddalena
frattanto siede presso la tavola. Sparafucile
beve dalla bottiglia lasciata dal Duca.
Rimangono ambidue taciturni per qualche
istante, e preoccupati da gravi pensieri)*

SPARAFUCILE

(Softly, to Maddalena)

Twenty golden scudi here.

(To the Duke)

I'd be happy to offer you my room.
If you'd like to,
We can go and see it now.

(Takes a lamp and goes up the stairs)

DUKE

Very well, I'm with you. Quickly, let's see it.

*(Speaks a word in Maddalena's ear, and
follows Sparafucile)*

MADDALENA

Poor young man, so gracious!
God, what a night this is!

DUKE

*(Up in the loft, seeing the unshuttered
windows)*

You sleep in the open air? Very well.
Good night.

SPARAFUCILE

May God protect you, sir.

DUKE

Let me sleep for a while; I'm tired.

Woman is as wayward
As a feather in the wind . . .

*(Takes off his hat and sword, and lies on the
bed where he quickly falls asleep. Meanwhile,
Maddalena sits by the table. Sparafucile drinks
from the bottle left by the Duke. Both are
silent for a few moments, preoccupied with
serious thoughts)*

MADDALENA

È amabile invero cotal giovinotto.

SPARAFUCILE

Oh sì, venti scudi ne dà di prodotto.

MADDALENA

Sol venti, son pochi, valeva di più.

SPARAFUCILE

La spada, s'ei dorme, va, portami, giù.

(Maddalena sale al granaio, ripara alla meglio il balcone e scende)

(Gilda comparisce nel fondo della via in costume virile, con stivali e speroni, e lentamente si avanza verso l'osteria, mentre Sparafucile continua a bere. Spessi lampi e tuoni)

GILDA

Ah, più non ragiono!
Amor mi trascina!
Mio padre, perdono.

(tuona)

Qual notte d'orrore!
Gran Dio, che accadrà?

MADDALENA

(sarà discesa ed avrà posata la spada del Duca sulla tavola)

Fratello?

GILDA

Chi parla?

(Osserva per la fessura)

SPARAFUCILE

(frugando in un credenzone)

Al diavol ten va.

MADDALENA

He's really charming, that young man.

SPARAFUCILE

Oh yes, he's earned twenty scudi for me.

MADDALENA

Only twenty. That's not much. He's worth more

SPARAFUCILE

His sword: if he's asleep, go and bring it to me.

(Maddalena goes up to the loft, sets things in order on the balcony, and returns)

(Gilda appears from the end of the street, in male clothes, wearing boots and spurs, and slowly approaches the inn, while Sparafucile continues drinking. The thunder and lightning continue)

GILDA

Ah, I can no longer reason!
Love brings me back here!
Father, forgive me.

(Thunder)

Such a night of horror!
Great God, what will happen?

MADDALENA

(Has come downstairs, and placed the Duke's sword on the table)

Brother?

GILDA

Who's speaking?

(Looks through a crack)

SPARAFUCILE

(Searching in a cupboard)

Go to the devil.

MADDALENA

Somiglia un Apollo quel giovine,
Io l'amo,
Ei m'ama, riposi,
Nè più l'uccidiamo.

GILDA

Oh cielo!

(ascoltando)

SPARAFUCILE

(gettandole un sacco)

Rattoppa quel sacco!

MADDALENA

Perché?

SPARAFUCILE

Entr'esso il tuo Apollo, sgozzato da me,
Gettar dovrò al fiume.

GILDA

L'inferno qui vedo!

MADDALENA

Eppure il danaro salvarti scommetto
Serbandolo in vita.

SPARAFUCILE

Difficile il credo.

MADDALENA

M'ascolta, anzi facil ti svelo un
progetto.
De' scudi già dieci dal gobbo ne avesti;
Venire cogli altri più tardi il vedrai.
Uccidilo . . .

GILDA

Che sento! Mio padre!

MADDALENA

That young man is like an Apollo.
I love him,
He loves me. Let him rest.
Let's not kill him.

GILDA

Oh heaven.

(Listening)

SPARAFUCILE

(Throwing a sack)

Mend that sack!

MADDALENA

Why?

SPARAFUCILE

I'll have to put your Apollo in it after
I've cut his throat,
And throw him in the river.

GILDA

Hell is here before my eyes.

MADDALENA

But the money I'm sure we can keep,
And yet let him live.

SPARAFUCILE

That's difficult to believe.

MADDALENA

Listen, and I'll reveal a simple plan.
You've already had ten scudi from the
hunchback.
You'll see him come back later with the rest.
Kill him . . .

GILDA

What do I hear? My father?

MADDALENA

. . . e venti allora ne avrai: Così
tutto il prezzo goder si potrà.

SPARAFUCILE

Uccider quel gobbo! Che diavol dicesti!
Un ladro son forse? Son forse un
bandito?
Qual altro cliente da me fu tradito!
Mi paga quest'uomo, fedele m'avrà.

MADDALENA

Ah, grazia per esso!

SPARAFUCILE

È d'uopo ch'ei muoia.

MADDALENA

Fuggire il fo adesso.

(*Va per salire*)

GILDA

Oh, buona figliuola!

SPARAFUCILE

(*trattenendola*)

Gli scudi perdiamo . . .

MADDALENA

È ver!

SPARAFUCILE

Lascia fare.

MADDALENA

Salvárlo dobbiamo.

SPARAFUCILE

Se pria ch'abbia il mezzo la notte
toccato
Alcuno qui giunga, per esso morrà.

MADDALENA

. . . And then you'll have the whole twenty:
In that way, you'll get the whole of your price.

SPARAFUCILE

Kill that hunchback? What the devil are
you saying?
Am I a thief, then? Or a bandit?
When have I ever betrayed a client?
This man has paid me, he shall have my fidelity.

MADDALENA

Ah, have mercy on him.

SPARAFUCILE

He must die.

MADDALENA

I'll warn him to flee now.

(*Goes to the staircase*)

GILDA

Oh, good girl!

SPARAFUCILE

(*Stopping her*)

We shall lose the money . . .

MADDALENA

That's true!

SPARAFUCILE

Let it happen.

MADDALENA

We must save him.

SPARAFUCILE

If, before midnight has struck,
Someone else should arrive, he can die
instead.

MADDALENA

È buia la notte, il ciel troppo irato,
Nessuno a quest'ora di qui passerà.

GILDA

Oh, qual tentazione! Morir per
l'ingrato?
Morire! E mio padre! O cielo, pietà!

(Battono le undici e mezzo)

SPARAFUCILE

Ancor c'è mezz'ora.

MADDALENA

(piangendo)

Attendi, fratello.

GILDA

Che! Piange tal donna!...
Nè a lui darò aita!
Ah, s'egli al mio amore divenne
rubello,
Io vo' per la sua gettar la mia vita.

(Picchia alla porta)

MADDALENA

Si picchia!

SPARAFUCILE

Fu il vento.

(Gilda torna a bussare)

MADDALENA

Si picchia, ti dico.

SPARAFUCILE

È strano!
Chi è?

MADDALENA

The night is dark, the sky too angry,
No one will pass by here at this hour.

GILDA

Oh, what a temptation! To die for the
ungrateful man?
To die! But my father! O heaven, pity!

(A clock strikes half past eleven)

SPARAFUCILE

There's half an hour to go.

MADDALENA

(Weeping)

Wait, brother.

GILDA

What, a woman such as that,
weeping?...
Shall I then not come to his aid?
Ah, although he has betrayed my love,
I shall lay down my life for his.

(She knocks at the door)

MADDALENA

Someone's knocking.

SPARAFUCILE

It was the wind.

(Gilda knocks again)

MADDALENA

There's someone knocking, I tell you.

SPARAFUCILE

That's strange!
Who is it?

GILDA

Pietà d'un mendico;
Asil per la notte a lui concedete.

MADDALENA

Fia lunga tal notte!

SPARAFUCILE

Alquanto attendete.

(Va a cercare nel credenzone)

MADDALENA

Su, spicciati, presto, fa l'opra compita:
Anelo una vita—con altra salvar.

SPARAFUCILE

Ebbene, son pronto; quell'uscio
dischiudi;
Più ch'altro gli scudi—mi preme salvar.

GILDA

Ah, presso alla morte sì giovine sono!
Oh ciel, per questi empî ti chieggo
perdono.
Perdona tu, o padre, a questa infelice!
Sia l'uomo felice—ch'or vado a salvar.

(bussa ancora)

MADDALENA

Spicciati.

SPARAFUCILE

Apri!

*(Va a postarsi con un pugnale dietro alla
porta; Maddalena apre e poi corre a chiudere
la grande arcata di fronte)*

MADDALENA

Entrate.

GILDA

Have pity on a beggar,
And give him shelter for the night.

MADDALENA

It will be a long night!

SPARAFUCILE

Wait a moment.

(He goes to search in the cupboard)

MADDALENA

Come on, hurry, be quick, get the job done:
I long to save one life by taking another.

SPARAFUCILE

Well, then, I'm ready; open that door;
More than any life, I'm interested in
saving my money.

GILDA

Ah, so young, I am about to die!
Oh heaven, I ask pardon for these villains.
And you, oh father, forgive your
unhappy daughter.
May that man be happy whom I now go
to save.

(Knocks again)

MADDALENA

Quickly.

SPARAFUCILE

Open!

*(He takes up his post behind the door, with a
dagger. Maddalena opens the door and then
quickly closes the front arcade gate)*

MADDALENA

Come in.

GILDA

(entra. Sparafucile chiude la porta dietro di lei. Tutto resta sepolto nel silenzio e nel buio)

Dio! Lor perdonate!

RIGOLETTO

(si avanza solo dal fondo della scena chiuso nel suo mantello. La violenza del temporale è diminuita, né più si vede e sente che qualche lampo e tuono)

Della vendetta alfin giunge l'istante!
Da trenta dì l'aspetto
Di vivo sangue a lagrime piangendo,
Sotto la larva del buffon. Quest'uscio . . .

(esaminando la casa)

È chiuso! Ah, non è tempo ancor!
S'attenda.
Qual notte di mistero!
Una tempesta in cielo!
In terra un omicidio!
Oh, come invero qui grande mi sento!

(Suona mezzanotte)

Mezzanotte!

(bussa alla porta)

(Sparafucile esce dalla casa)

SPARAFUCILE

Chi è là?

RIGOLETTO

(per entrare)

Son io.

SPARAFUCILE

Sostate.

(Rientra e torna trascinando un sacco)

È qua spento il vostr'uomo!

GILDA

(Enters. Sparafucile closes the door behind her. All is now buried in silence and darkness)

God, forgive them!

RIGOLETTO

(Enters from the back of the scene, wrapped in his cloak. The violence of the storm has diminished, and there is only occasional thunder and lightning)

The moment of vengeance at last has arrived.
For thirty days I've awaited it,
Weeping tears of blood
Beneath the jester's mask. This is the door . . .

(Examining the house)

It's shut. Ah, it's not time yet,
I'll wait.
What a night of mystery!
A tempest in the heavens!
On earth a murder!
Oh! how really powerful I feel now!

(Midnight strikes)

Midnight!

(He knocks at the door)

(Sparafucile comes out of the house)

SPARAFUCILE

Who's there.

RIGOLETTO

(About to enter)

It's I.

SPARAFUCILE

Wait.

(He goes inside, and returns dragging a sack)

Here's your man, dead!

RIGOLETTO

Oh gioia! . . . Un lume!

SPARAFUCILE

Un lume? No, il danaro.

(*Rigoletto gli dà una borsa*)

Lesti all'onda il gettiam.

RIGOLETTO

No, basto io solo.

SPARAFUCILE

Come vi piace. Qui men atto è il sito.
Più avanti è più profondo il gorgo.
Presto,
Che alcun non vi sorprenda. Buona
notte.

(*Rientra in casa*)

RIGOLETTO

Egli è là! Morto!
Oh sì! Vorrei vederlo!
Ma che importa? È ben desso!
Ecco i suoi sproni.
Ora mi guarda, o mondo!
Quest'è un buffone, ed un potente è
questo!
Ei sta sotto i miei piedi! È desso! Oh
gioia!
È giunta alfine la tua vendetta, o duolo!
Sia l'onda a lui sepolcro,
Un sacco il suo lenzuolo! All'onda!
All'onda!

(*Fa per trascinare il sacco verso la sponda,
quando è sorpreso dalla lontana voce del
Duca, che nel fondo attraversa la scena*)

DUCA

La donna è mobile . . .

RIGOLETTO

Oh joy . . . A light!

SPARAFUCILE

A light? No, give me my money.

(*Rigoletto gives him a purse*)

Quick, let's throw him in the river.

RIGOLETTO

No, I'll do it alone.

SPARAFUCILE

As you please. This place is not so
suitable.
Further on the river is deeper. Quickly,
Before anyone comes to disturb you.
Good night.

(*Goes back into the house*)

RIGOLETTO

There he is! Dead!
Oh yes, I must see him!
What does it matter. It's he, all right.
Here are his spurs.
Look at me now, oh world!
This is a jester, and that a potentate!
He lies beneath my feet. It's he! Oh,
joy!
Oh sorrow, your revenge has arrived at
last!
Let the waves be his sepulchre,
A sack his shroud. Into the river! Into
the river!

(*As he is about to drag the sack towards the
river, he is amazed to hear in the distance the
voice of the Duke who crosses the rear of the scene*)

DUKE

Woman is as wayward . . .

RIGOLETTO

Qual voce! Illusion notturna è questa!

(trasalendo)

No! No! Egli è desso!

(verso la casa)

Maledizione! Olà! Dimon bandito!

(taglia il sacco)

Chi è mai, chi è qui in sua vece?
Io tremo. È umano corpo!

(Lampeggia)

Mia figlia! Dio! Mia figlia!
Ah no . . . è impossibil!
Per Verona è in via!

(inginocchiandosi)

Fu visïon! E dessa!
O mia Gilda: fanciulla, a me rispondi!
L'assassino mi svela. Olà? Nessuno?

(Picchia disperatamente alla porta.)

Nessun! Mia figlia! Mia Gilda!

GILDA

Chi mi chiama?

RIGOLETTO

Ella parla! Si muove!
È viva! Oh Dio!
Ah, mio ben solo in terra . . .
Mi guarda, mi conosci?

GILDA

Ah, padre mio!

RIGOLETTO

Qual mistero! Che fu?
Sei tu ferita? Dimmi!

RIGOLETTO

That voice! This is some nocturnal illusion!

(With a start)

No, no, it's he!

(Turning to the house)

Curse you! Hey there! Fiendish robber!

(Cuts open the sack)

But who is it, who is it in his place?
I tremble. It's a human body!

(A flash of lightning)

My daughter! God! My daughter!
Ah no . . . it's impossible. She's on her
way to Verona!

(Kneeling)

It was a vision! It's she!
Oh my Gilda, daughter, speak to me!
Tell me who the assassin was. Hey
there. Is no one there?

(Knocks desperately at the door)

No one! My daughter! My Gilda!

GILDA

Who is calling me?

RIGOLETTO

She speaks! She moves!
She's alive! Oh God!
Ah, my only joy on earth . . .
Look at me. Do you know me?

GILDA

Ah, my father!

RIGOLETTO

What a mystery! What happened?
Are you wounded? Tell me.

GILDA

L'acciar qui mi piagò.

(indicando al core)

RIGOLETTO

Chi t'ha colpita?

GILDA

V'ho ingannato, colpevole fui,
L'amai troppo, ora muoio per lui!

RIGOLETTO

(tra sé)

Dio tremendo! Ella stessa fu côlta
Dallo stral di mia giusta vendetta!

(forte)

Angiol caro! Mi guarda, m'ascolta,
Parla, parlami, figlia diletta.

GILDA

Ah, ch'io taccia, a me, a lui perdonate,
Benedite alla figlia, o mio padre.
Lassù, in cielo, vicina alla madre,
In eterno per voi pregherò.

RIGOLETTO

Non morir, mio tesoro, pietate!
Mia colomba, lasciarmi non dêi.
Se t'involi, qui sol rimarrei.
Non morire, o qui teco morrò!

GILDA

Non più. A lui perdonate,
Mio padre, addio!

(muore)

RIGOLETTO

Gilda! Mia Gilda! È morta!
Ah, la maledizione!

(Cade sul cadavere della figlia)

GILDA

The knife pierced me here.

(She points to her heart)

RIGOLETTO

Who struck the blow?

GILDA

I deceived you, I was to blame.
I loved him too much, now I'm dying for him!

RIGOLETTO

(To himself)

Almighty God! She herself was struck
By the arrow of my just vengeance!

(Aloud)

Dear angel! Look at me, listen to me,
Speak, speak to me, my darling daughter.

GILDA

Ah, let me be. Forgive me, and him.
Bless your daughter, oh my father.
Up there, in heaven, close to my mother,
In eternity I shall pray for you.

RIGOLETTO

Do not die, my beloved, have pity!
My dove, you mustn't leave me.
If you fly away, I should be left here alone.
Do not die, or let me die with you.

GILDA

No more. Forgive him.
My father, farewell.

(She dies)

RIGOLETTO

Gilda! My Gilda! She's dead!
Ah, the curse!

(He falls on his daughter's corpse)

CURTAIN

Chronology

1813   Born on October 10, in the village of Le Roncole, near Parma, where his father was the inn-keeper. At first taught music by the local organist, and at the age of ten went to the nearest town, Busseto, to continue his studies. He lodged in the house of a merchant, Antonio Barezzi, who helped him eventually to get to Milan where he hoped to study at the Conservatorium.

1832   Rejected by the Conservatorium as being over age for admittance, the nineteen-year-old composer studied privately.

1836   Married his benefactor Barezzi's daughter, Margherita.

1837   Began to write his first opera, *Oberto*. A daughter, Virginia, born on March 26.

1838   A son, Icilio, born on July 11. Virginia died on August 12, at the age of sixteen months.

1839   Icilio died on October 22, aged fifteen months. *Oberto* was performed at La Scala Opera House, Milan, on November 17, and was warmly received.

1840   While Verdi was at work on a second opera, *Un giorno di regno*, his wife Margherita died on June 18. *Un giorno di regno*, a comic opera, failed miserably at La Scala at its first performance on September 5. Verdi, crushed by his family tragedies and his professional failure, wanted to give up operatic composition and return to Busseto, but was persuaded by Merelli, the Scala impresario, to undertake a third opera, *Nabucco*, based on the Old Testament story of Nebuchadnezzar.

1842   *Nabucco*, performed at La Scala on March 9, was an overwhelming success, and Verdi's future as a composer of opera was assured. The young country lad soon became sought after in the salons of Milan, but, introspective and inclined to melancholy, preferred work to social life. For the next ten years, he composed operas on commission at the rate of one and sometimes two a year.

1843   *I Lombardi* performed at La Scala, February 11. *Ernani* commissioned by Teatro La Fenice, Venice.

1844   *Ernani* performed at La Fenice, March 9. *I due Foscari* performed at Teatro Argentina, Rome, November 3.

1845   *Giovanna d'Arco* performed at La Scala, February 15, after which, dissatisfied with that theatre's standards and with the management's treatment of him, Verdi broke off relations with La Scala. *Alzira* performed at the Teatro San Carlo, Naples, on August 12.

1846   *Attila* performed at La Fenice, Venice, on March 17. Verdi, suffering from nervous exhaustion, was ordered six months' complete rest. A staunch local patriot, he allied himself, early in his career, to the liberal cause in politics, and to the movement known as the *risorgimento* which eventually was to lead to the unification of Italy. During the years of disunity and of Austrian occupation of much of northern Italy, Verdi's audiences tended to identify many of his early operas as rallying cries for a united Italy, and Verdi was quite willing to be thought of as the composer of the *risorgimento*.

1847   *Macbeth* performed in Florence on March 14, after which Verdi travelled to London for the première on July 22 of *I masnadieri* which he had composed for Her Majesty's Theatre. While in Paris, en route to London, he renewed acquaintance with the soprano Giuseppina Strepponi whom he had first met in his early days in Milan and who had sung in the first performances of *Nabucco*. They became lovers, and were to live together for twelve years before eventually marrying.

1848   *Il corsaro* performed in Trieste, on October 25.

1849   *La battaglia di Legnano*, Verdi's one overtly patriotic opera, performed in Rome on January 27. After living for a time in Paris with Giuseppina Strepponi, Verdi returned to his house at Busseto, bringing Giuseppina with him. Travelled to Naples for the première of *Luisa Miller* on December 8.

1850   *Stiffelio* performed in Trieste on November 16.

1851   *Rigoletto* performed at La Fenice, Venice, on March 11. Verdi and Giuseppina spent the winter of 1851–52 in Paris.

1853   *Il trovatore* performed in Rome on January 19, and *La traviata* at La Fenice, Venice, on March 6. *La traviata* initially a failure, due mainly to poor performance. A second production the following year established the opera's immense success. Having purchased a villa and farm at Sant' Agata, outside Busseto, Verdi now began to divide his time between Sant' Agata and Paris, where he had been commissioned to write a work for the Paris Opéra.

1855   *Les Vêpres siciliennes* performed at the Paris Opéra on June 13.

1857   *Simon Boccanegra* performed at La Fenice, Venice, on March 12. At Rimini on August 16, Verdi supervised the production of *Aroldo*, a revised version of *Stiffelio* with a completely new last act. *Un ballo in maschera* composed for Naples.

1858   Due to difficulties created by the Neapolitan censorship authorities, *Un ballo in maschera* was not produced in Naples, and Verdi offered the work to Rome.

1859   *Un ballo in maschera* performed in Rome on February 17. On August 29, Verdi and Giuseppina Strepponi were married in the small town of Collonges-sous-Salève, near the Swiss border.

1861   When the first free Italian parliament was instituted in 1860, Verdi reluctantly agreed to stand for election. He was duly elected to the Italian legislative assembly, and was to serve assiduously for five years although he found political office irksome.

1862   In the winter of 1861–62, the Verdis travelled to Russia for the production of *La forza del destino* which Verdi had composed for the Imperial Opera at St Petersburg. The illness of the leading soprano caused a postponement of the première, and the Verdis travelled via Berlin and Paris to London, where Verdi was representing Italy at an international exhibition. They returned to St Petersburg in the autumn of 1862, and *La forza del destino* was given its first performance there on November 10.

1865   Verdi revised his 1847 *Macbeth* for production in Paris, and the revised opera had its première on April 21. Verdi accepted a commission to compose a new work for the Opéra, to be performed during the Paris Exhibition of 1867.

1867   *Don Carlos* performed at the Paris Opéra March 11.

1868   In Milan, Verdi met for the first time one of his heroes, the novelist Alessandro Manzoni.

1869   Opening of the Suez Canal. As part of the celebrations the Cairo Opera House was opened, with Verdi's *Rigoletto*.

1870   Verdi agreed to write an opera for Cairo.

1871   *Aida* was performed in Cairo on December 24.

1873   The death of Manzoni led Verdi to compose a Requiem Mass in his memory.

1874   Verdi's Requiem Mass for Manzoni was given its first performance in a Milan church on May 22, and subsequently taken on a European tour by Verdi who conducted all the performances.

1879   Considering himself at least semi-retired, Verdi now spent most of his time either in Sant' Agata or in his apartment in Genoa. His publisher, however, engineered a meeting between Verdi and Arrigo Boito, the poet and composer whom Verdi had first met nearly twenty years earlier. Verdi agreed to collaborate with Boito on a revision of *Simon Boccanegra*.

1881   The revised *Simon Boccanegra* was performed at La Scala, Milan, on March 24. Verdi now reluctantly agreed to attempt to compose a completely new opera to a libretto by Boito. The subject chosen was Shakespeare's *Othello*. Verdi worked slowly and intermittently on the opera.

1887   *Otello* was produced, to great acclaim, at La Scala, on February 5. In the opinion of many, it was the seventy-three-year-old composer's finest opera. Verdi and Boito were immediately urged to begin another opera, but Verdi was not to be rushed, and began to devote more of his time to his various philanthropic concerns.

1889   The fiftieth anniversary of Verdi's first opera, *Oberto*, which was revived at La Scala on November 17. Verdi and Boito began work on *Falstaff*.

1893   In its composer's eightieth year, *Falstaff* was completed and given its première at La Scala on February 9.

1894   Verdi travelled to Paris for the French première of *Otello*, for which he composed ballet music.

1897   Giuseppina died of pneumonia on November 14. Alone and desolate, Verdi found comfort, or at least distraction, in setting up his Rest Home for Aged Musicians in Milan. He spent Christmas, 1900, visiting his adopted daughter in Milan.

1901   At the Grand Hotel, Milan, Verdi succumbed to a sudden stroke on January 21, and died on January 27. He was eighty-seven years of age.

Major Compositions by Verdi

(The dates in brackets are those of first performances)

Operas

Oberto (1839)
Un giorno di regno (1840)
Nabucco (1842)
I Lombardi (1843) (French version, *Jérusalem*, 1847)
Ernani (1844)
I due Foscari (1844)
Giovanna d'Arco (1845)
Alzira (1845)
Attila (1846)
Macbeth (1847) (revised version, 1865)
I masnadieri (1847)
Il corsaro (1848)
La battaglia di Legnano (1849)
Luisa Miller (1849)
Stiffelio (1850) (revised version, *Aroldo*, 1857)
Rigoletto (1851)
Il trovatore (1853)
La traviata (1853)
Les Vêpres siciliennes (1855)
Simon Boccanegra (1857) (revised version, 1881)
Un ballo in maschera (1859)
La forza del destino (1862) (revised version, 1869)
Don Carlos (1867) (revised Italian version, *Don Carlo*, 1884)
Aida (1871)
Otello (1887)
Falstaff (1893)

Choral Works

Inno delle Nazioni (1862)
Messa da Requiem (1874)
Quatto Pezzi Sacri (1898, ii to iv only)
    (i) *Ave Maria*; (ii) *Stabat mater*; (iii) *Laudi alla Vergine Maria*;
    (iv) *Te Deum*

Chamber Music

String Quartet in E minor (1873)

Suggested Further Reading

Budden, Julian: *The Operas of Verdi* (London, Vol I, 1973; Vol 2, 1978)

Godefroy, Vincent: *The Dramatic Genius of Verdi* (London, Vol I, 1975; Vol II, 1977)

Hughes, Spike: *Famous Verdi Operas* (London, 1968)

Martin, George: *Verdi, His Music, Life and Times* (New York, 1963)

Osborne, Charles: *The Complete Operas of Verdi* (London, 1969)

Osborne, Charles (ed.): *Letters of Giuseppe Verdi* (London, 1971)

Osborne, Charles: *Verdi* (London, 1978)

Toye, Francis: *Giuseppe Verdi, His Life and Works* (London 1931)

Walker, Frank: *The Man Verdi* (London, 1962)

Acknowledgments

The illustrations are reproduced by kind permission of the following: BBC Broadcasting House: 6; British Library (Photo: Ray Gardner): 33, 36, 37, 85; Donald Southern: 53, 79; Doreen and Sidney Spellman Collection: 21, 87; Foto Tosi: 13, 16, 22 (left); Harold Rosenthal: 77; Houston Rogers: 54, 74, 75, 76; J. Heffernan, Metropolitan Opera: 56, 70; John Garner: 80; Louis Mélancon, New York: 57; Mander and Mitcheson: 86; The Mansell Collection: 24; Mary Evans Picture Library: 26, 29; Metropolitan Opera Archives: 55, 60, 61, 62–3, 64, 67, 71, 72, 83, 90; Nancy Sorensen, Lyric Opera of Chicago: 68; Osvaldo Bohm, Venice: 51; Peyer, Hamburg: 59, 92; Radio Times Hulton Picture Library: 9, 11, 52, 89, 95, 96, 98; Reginald Davis: 48, 49; Rudolf Betz, Munich: 93; Sadler's Wells Opera: 58; Teatro la Fenice, Venice (lent by Weidenfeld & Nicolson picture archives): 19, 25, 46, 47.